WORKBOOK 4

B2

Herbert Puchta, Jeff Stranks & Peter Lewis-Jones

CAMBRIDGE
UNIVERSITY PRESS

Acknowledgements

The authors and publishers acknowledge the following sources of copyright material and are grateful for the permissions granted. While every effort has been made, it has not always been possible to identify the sources of all the material used, or to trace all copyright holders. If any omissions are brought to our notice, we will be happy to include the appropriate acknowledgements on reprinting and in the next update to the digital edition, as applicable.

National Geographic Creative for the text on p. 14 adapted from 'Instants: Dispatches from the Dawn Wall' by Mallory Benedict & 'Duo Completes First Free Climb of Yosemite's Dawn Wall, Making History' by Andrew Bisharat. Copyright © 2015 National Geographic Creative. Reproduced with permission;

Eurosport for the text on p. 27 adapted from 'Quick-thinking golf star saves own life after potentially fatal spider bite' by Bunker Mentality. Copyright © Eurosport. Reproduced with permission;

The Independent for the text on p. 58 adapted from 'Mugging victim Alan Barnes plans to move house after donations reach £200,000', *The Independent* 02.02.2015. Copyright © The Independent;

Northern and Shell Media Publications for the text on p. 58 adapted from 'Dozens of police and firefighters surprise autistic boy after classmates all miss party' by Sarah Ann Harris. Copyright © Northern and Shell Media Publications. Reproduced by kind permission;

Text on p. 63 adapted from 'Boy drops phone on fishing trip, drains entire pond to find it' by Valerie Loftus, *TheJournal.ie*, 03.08.2014;

St. Martin's Press for the text on p. 86 adapted from *The Teen's Guide to World Domination: Advice on Life, Liberty, and the Pursuit of Awesomeness* by Josh Shipp. Copyright © 2010 St. Martin's Press. Reproduced with permission of Macmillan;

Text on p. 112 adapted from 'Urban Exploration Photographer Finds a Stash of Cash in an Abandoned House' by Michael Zhang. Copyright © PetaPixel;

Text on p. 113 adapted from '13 of history's greatest polar explorers' by Laura Moss, http://www.mnn.com/earth-matters/animals/photos/13-of-historys-greatest-polar-explorers/ann-bancroft. Copyright © Narrative Content Group.

Corpus
Development of this publication has made use of the Cambridge English Corpus (CEC). The CEC is a computer database of contemporary spoken and written English, which currently stands at over one billion words. It includes British English, American English and other varieties of English. It also includes the Cambridge Learner Corpus, developed in collaboration with Cambridge English Language Assessment. Cambridge University Press has built up the CEC to provide evidence about language use that helps to produce better language teaching materials.

English Profile
This product is informed by the English Vocabulary Profile, built as part of English Profile, a collaborative programme designed to enhance the learning, teaching and assessment of English worldwide. Its main funding partners are Cambridge University Press and Cambridge English Language Assessment and its aim is to create a 'profile' for English linked to the Common European Framework of Reference for Languages (CEF). English Profile outcomes, such as the English Vocabulary Profile, will provide detailed information about the language that learners can be expected to demonstrate at each CEF level, offering a clear benchmark for learners' proficiency. For more information, please visit www.englishprofile.org

Cambridge Dictionaries
Cambridge dictionaries are the world's most widely used dictionaries for learners of English. The dictionaries are available in print and online at dictionary.cambridge.org. Copyright © Cambridge University Press, reproduced with permission.

The publishers are grateful to the following for permission to reproduce copyright photographs and material:

T = Top, B = Below, L = Left, R = Right, C = Centre, B/G = Background

p. 6 (TL): ©lithian/Shutterstock; p. 6 (TR): ©Chris Whitehead/Cultura/Getty Images; p. 6 (CL): ©dogist/Shutterstock; p. 6 (CR): ©Anneka/Shutterstock; p. 6 (BL): ©Robert Hoetink/Alamy Stock Photo; p. 6 (BR): ©Jon Feigersh/Blend Images/Getty Images; p. 10: ©Jennika Argent/Moment Open/Getty Images; p. 12: ©Tracy Whiteside/Shutterstock; p. 14: ©Corey Rich/Aurora/Getty Images; p. 15: ©Kevin Foy/Alamy Stock Photo; p. 22: ©wjarek/Shutterstock; p. 23: ©mffoto/Shutterstock; p. 24: ©Andrea Willmore/Shutterstock; p. 25: ©Hero Images/Getty Images; p. 26: ©Tuul and Bruno Morandi/The Image Bank/Getty Images; p. 27 (L): ©Paul Mason/Shutterstock; p. 27 (R): ©Don Farrall/DigitalVision/Getty Images; p. 31 (a): ©Robyn Mackenzie/Shutterstock; p. 31 (b): ©OZaiachin/Shutterstock; p. 31 (c): ©nito/Shutterstock; p. 31 (d): ©Andrey_Kuzmin/Shutterstock; p. 31 (e): ©kedrov/Shutterstock; p. 31 (f): ©homydesign/Shutterstock; p. 31 (g): ©Sibrikov Valery/Shutterstock; p. 31 (h): ©BJI/Blue Jean Images/Getty Images; p. 31 (i): ©Brooke Becker/Shutterstock; p. 33: ©Tania Kolinko/Shutterstock; p. 35 (T): ©Goodluz/Shutterstock; p. 35 (B): ©michaeljung/Shutterstock; p. 36: ©Cultura RM/Craig Easton/Getty Images; p. 40: ©Fred Stein Archive/Archive Photos/Getty Images; p. 44: ©Golden Pixels LLC/Alamy Stock Photo; p. 49 (a): ©anaken2012/Shutterstock; p. 49 (b): ©Nikita Rogul/Shutterstock; p. 49 (c): ©Pavel Kubarkov/Shutterstock; p. 49 (d): ©KonstantinChristian/Shutterstock; p. 49 (e): ©Vladimir Mucibabic/Shutterstock; p. 49 (f): ©Olga Popova/Shutterstock; p. 55: ©Edyta Pawlowska/Shutterstock; p. 57: ©Kevin Moore/Alamy Stock Photo; p. 58: ©Ian Forsyth/Getty Images; p. 59 (T): ©Goodluz/Shutterstock; p. 59 (B): ©Ann Summa/Corbis; p. 68 (T): ©NEW LINE/DARK HORSE/THE KOBAL COLLECTION; p. 68 (C): ©De Agostini Picture Library/Getty Images; p. 68 (B): ©ZORAN BOZICEVIC/AFP/Getty Images; p. 76 (L): ©Graham Wood/Associated Newspapers/REX Shutterstock; p. 76 (R): ©Sam Camp/iStock/Getty Images Plus/Getty Images; p. 77: ©Latitudestock/Gallo Images/Getty Images; p. 78: ©Kali Nine LLC/E+/Getty Images; p. 79 (L): ©Peter Phipp/Travelshots.com/Alamy Stock Photo; p. 79 (R): ©Realimage/Alamy Stock Photo; p. 80 (a): ©Paul Orr/Shutterstock; p. 80 (b): ©Natalia Siverina/Shutterstock; p. 80 (c): ©BranislavP/Shutterstock; p. 80 (d): ©Skoda/Shutterstock; p. 80 (e): ©Radu Razvan/Shutterstock; p. 80 (f): ©Don Pablo/Shutterstock; p. 83: ©Dragan Grkic/iStock/Getty Images Plus/Getty Images; p. 86: ©Syda Productions/Shutterstock; p. 88 (T): ©pbombaert/Shutterstock; p. 88 (C): ©urbanbuzz/Shutterstock; p. 88 (B): ©Inna Astakhova/Shutterstock; p. 90: ©Sutichak Yachiangkham/Shutterstock; p. 94: ©oliveromg/Shutterstock; p. 104 (TL): ©UNIVERSAL/THE KOBAL COLLECTION; p. 104 (TR): ©COLUMBIA/THE KOBAL COLLECTION/SCHWARTZ, ANDY; p. 104 (BL): ©DREAMWORKS/PARAMOUNT/THE KOBAL COLLECTION/CONNOR, FRANK; p. 104 (BR): ©TRI-STAR/WINGNUT/SONY/THE KOBAL COLLECTION; p. 105: ©DREAMWORKS ANIMATION/20TH CENTURY FOX/THE KOBAL COLLECTION; p. 112 (L): ©Nir Levy/Shutterstock; p. 112 (R): ©Ian Paterson/Alamy Stock Photo; p. 113: Courtesy of Bancroft Arnesen Explore, www.annbancroftfoundation.org and www.yourexpedition.com; p. 117: ©UNIVERSAL/DOUGLAS/GRUSKOFF PRODUCTIONS/THE KOBAL COLLECTION.

Cover photographs by: (TL): ©Stephen Moore/Digital Vision Vectors/Getty Images; (BL): ©Pete Starman/Stone/Getty Images; (C): ©imagedb.com/Shutterstock; (TR): ©Stephen Moore/Digital Vision Vectors/Getty Images; (BR): ©Kimberley Coole/Lonely Planet Images/Getty Images.

The publishers are grateful to the following illustrators:
David Semple 29, 42, 60, 73, 82, 103, 108
Julian Mosedale 5, 34, 50, 67, 100, 106
Blooberry 107

The publishers are grateful to the following contributors:
Blooberry: text design and layouts; Hilary Fletcher: picture research; Leon Chambers: audio recordings; Karen Elliott: Pronunciation sections; Rebecca Raynes: Get it right! exercises

CONTENTS

WELCOME

A WHAT A STORY!

Descriptive verbs

1 **Choose the correct options to complete the sentences.**

1 The hurricane *demolished / fled / raged* everything in its path.
2 The prisoner *struck / smashed / dived* under the water to escape the bullets.
3 The family *smashed / fled / struck* from their burning home.
4 As she started to fall I managed to *grab / rage / scream* her by the arm.
5 The fire *demolished / raged / dived* through the trees.
6 The people *screamed / grabbed / demolished* in terror as the wave came towards them.
7 The robbers *smashed / flew / screamed* down a wall to break into the bank.
8 The car was *grabbed / dived / struck* by the falling tree.

Phrasal verbs

1 **Complete the sentences with the correct form of the verbs in the list.**

end | sort | stand | take
look | break | give | carry

1 I think I might _____ up yoga. It's really good for body and mind.
2 He studied medicine at university so I'm not sure how he _____ up as an accountant.
3 Can you believe it? Our car _____ down five miles from home.
4 I know I should _____ up eating so much chocolate but I think I'd find it too difficult.
5 They _____ on eating their picnic even though it started to rain.
6 When I have a problem my mum always helps me _____ it out.
7 I'm really _____ forward to the summer holidays. I need a rest.
8 Bill really _____ out in the class photo because he's so tall.

Elements of a story

1 **Match the words with the definitions.**

1 hero ☐
2 plot ☐
3 dialogue ☐
4 characters ☐
5 ending ☐
6 opening ☐
7 villain ☐
8 setting ☐

a the people in the story
b a bad man or woman
c how the story starts
d how the story finishes
e the man or woman in the story we identify with
f the place where the story happens
g what the people in the story say
h the storyline

2 **Complete the text with the missing words.**

So what do you need to write a successful story? Well to start with you need a good ¹_____ – without a great story you've got no chance. Of course any good story needs a selection of different ²_____, a ³_____ for the reader to identify with and a ⁴_____ to hate. And to help bring all these people alive you'll need to have good ⁵_____ between them. What they say and how they say it is so important. Then you'll need a ⁶_____ for your story. Where and when does the action happen? Is it the modern day, in the past or even in the future?

So now you've got all that, it's time to start writing. The ⁷_____ is essential. You'll need to get your reader's attention from the very beginning. And once you've got their attention hopefully they'll read right through so you'll need to give them a good ⁸_____ too, to make sure they won't feel they've wasted their time.

And that's all you need. That and a lot of luck.

Talking about past routines

1 ◁))02 **Listen and put the pictures in order.**

2 **Complete the sentences so they are true for you.**

1 When I was really young my mum/dad would

2 My first teacher at school used to

3 When I was upset I used to

4 When it was my birthday, my parents would

5 During the school holidays I would

SUMMING UP

1 **Put the dialogue in order.**

☐ ANA Well, for example, he'd tell a story about how a fire was raging through our house and how we needed to smash down the door. And he'd do all the actions.

1 ANA My dad used to tell me really great stories when I was a kid.

☐ ANA Yes it is. I really miss his stories.

☐ ANA Really dramatic and exciting stories, and he would pretend they were happening to us.

☐ ANA He was. I used to really look forward to his stories. But he gave up telling them as I got older.

☐ JAKE That's a shame.

☐ JAKE What kind of stories?

☐ JAKE He sounds like a really fun dad.

☐ JAKE What do you mean?

B AN UNCERTAIN FUTURE
Future plans

1 **Match the sentence halves.**

1 I don't leave ☐
2 You'll need to get a ☐
3 Many young people are waiting longer to start ☐
4 Before I start my career I'd love to travel ☐
5 I'd like to make enough money so I can ☐
6 My parents would love me to settle ☐

a a family these days.
b the world for a year or so.
c retire before I'm 60.
d down but I'm not ready yet.
e school for another two years.
f really good degree if you want to work for them.

Life plans

1 **Put the events in the order that they happened.**

☐ So I returned home and started doing a degree.

☐ So I decided to travel the world for a while until I made up my mind.

☐ When I was in Asia I suddenly realised what career I wanted to do – teaching.

☐ We started a family after I had been teaching for a few years.

1 When I left school I wasn't too sure what I wanted to do.

☐ Next year I'm going to retire. I can't help wondering how it all passed so quickly.

☐ After the birth of my second son, I got promoted. I'm now a head teacher.

☐ In my final year of university I met the love of my life and we settled down.

Future continuous

1 **Complete the sentences using the future continuous form of the verb in brackets.**

Two months from now …

1 I _____ on a sunny beach in Greece. (lie)
2 I _____ exams anymore. (not do)
3 I _____ delicious food every night. (eat)
4 I _____ every morning at 6 am! (not get up)
5 I _____ in a 5-star hotel. (stay)
6 I _____ the bus to school every morning. (not take)

I can't wait for the summer holidays!

Being emphatic: *so* and *such*

1 Choose the correct option.

1 This exercise is *so / such* difficult.

2 Mr Peters is *so / such* a good teacher.

3 That was *so / such* a bad game of football.

4 I was *so / such* late for school today.

5 She gave me *so / such* a great present.

6 Andrew is *so / such* good at chess.

7 I feel *so / such* tired today.

8 We had *so / such* a good holiday.

2 Complete the sentences with *so* or *such*. Then match the sentences to the photos.

1 It's _____ a smart dog. ☐

2 They're _____ a talented family. ☐

3 I really am _____ tired. ☐

4 It's _____ windy today. ☐

5 They're _____ a bad team. ☐

6 This cake is _____ delicious. ☐

A

B

C

D

E

F

Extreme adjectives

1 Complete with the missing adjectives.

0 That film wasn't bad. It was t *errible*   !

1 I don't find Maths interesting. I find it f_____!

2 That joke wasn't funny. It was h_____!

3 The water's not cold. It's f_____!

4 No, they weren't scared. They were t_____!

5 Their house isn't big. It's e_____!

6 That dog isn't small. It's t_____!

7 It isn't hot today. It's b_____!

2 Complete the second diary entry with extreme adjectives.

> 01/01/1996
>
> Life's pretty good. I can't really complain. I live in a big house with my parents. We get on well most of the time. I like school. It's interesting and I really enjoy going most days. Mr Henderson, my Science teacher, is really funny. He makes me laugh and it's always fun in his lessons. In my spare time I go go-karting. It's a really exciting hobby. I won a trophy last week. It was pretty small but the size isn't important. It says 'Most Improved Driver' on it so I'm happy with it. I'm not sure my mum's so keen on my hobby. She's scared I'll have an accident. I tell her not to worry and that one day I'll be a world champion.

> 02/02/2016
>
> Life's pretty ¹_____. I can't complain at all. I live in a ²_____ house with my wife and children. We get on well all of the time. I like my job. It's ³_____ and I really enjoy going most days. My boss is really ⁴_____. He makes me laugh and it's always fun hanging out with him. I'm a racing driver. It's a really ⁵_____ sport. I won a trophy last week. It was ⁶_____ but the size isn't important. It says 'World Champion' on it so I'm ⁷_____ with it. I'm not sure my mum's so keen on my job. She's ⁸_____ I'll have an accident. I tell her, 'Isn't it time you stopped worrying?'

SUMMING UP

1 Complete the dialogue with the words in the list. There are four extra words.

amazing | settle | terrible | promote
degree | enormous | so | such
retire | career | travel | huge

KATIE So what are your plans for the weekend, Conner?

CONNER Well my dad's going to ¹_____ from work next week so we're having an ²_____ party for him on Saturday. I mean it's going to be really big!

KATIE But he's ³_____ young!

CONNER I know, and the crazy thing is that the company offered to ⁴_____ him too.

KATIE So what made him decide to leave?

CONNER Well the money he got was ⁵_____ but it was ⁶_____ a stressful job.

KATIE Yes, money isn't everything.

CONNER Now he's got plans to ⁷_____ the world with Mum.

KATIE But what about you?

CONNER Well, I hope they're going to wait until I'm at university doing a ⁸_____. But the mood Dad's in, I can't be too sure!

C HOW PEOPLE BEHAVE

Personality

1 Complete the descriptions with adjectives.

1 He only thinks about himself and what's good for him. He's really s_____.

2 She always says 'please' or 'thank you'. She's very p_____.

3 You didn't need to buy me a present. That was very t_____ of you.

4 He never panics. He's a very c_____ person.

5 She's very l_____. She always seems to have so much energy.

6 He's very quiet, not because he's unfriendly, he's just a bit s_____.

7 He's very g_____ with both his money and, more importantly, his time.

8 He left without saying 'goodbye', which I thought was a bit r_____.

Using *should*

1 Write a reply. Use *should* or *shouldn't*.

0 'I'm really tired today.'
   You should have gone to bed earlier.

1 'It's Luis's birthday tomorrow.'
   _____

2 'I can't believe it. We've missed the bus.'
   _____

3 'My tooth is really hurting.'
   _____

4 'Mia's really upset with me.'
   _____

5 'I'm bored.'
   _____

2 Complete the dialogue with *should / shouldn't have* and the correct form of the verbs in the list.

stay | get up | bring | put | set

TEACHER Have you done your homework, Elsie?

ELSIE Umm, I have but I left it at home.

TEACHER But it was for today. You [1]_____ it with you.

ELSIE I know. I'm sorry but I was in such a hurry I left it on the kitchen table.

TEACHER You [2]_____ earlier. Then you wouldn't have been in such a hurry.

ELSIE I know. I [3]_____ my alarm clock but I forgot. And I [4]_____ my book in my bag the night before. And I [5]_____ up so late last night.

Career paths

1 Use the clues to complete the crossword and find the mystery profession.

1 They take all the rubbish from the roads.

2 My brother builds bridges and tunnels.

3 She tries to help people who find themselves in trouble with the police.

4 She looks after a 4-year-old and two 6-year-olds.

5 My aunt works in a really busy hospital in the middle of London.

6 He gets us to and from school.

2 Choose the correct option.

1 My aunt is a receptionist at the clinic. She works in *finance / healthcare*.

2 My whole family work in *public service / management*. Dad's a nurse, Mum's a teacher and my uncle is a policeman.

3 I'd like to work in *law / education*, maybe as a professor at a university.

4 If you want to get into medical school you'll need the right *qualifications / salary*.

5 There are more than 500 *employees / employers* working at the factory.

6 They're one of the biggest *employees / employers* in the region with more than 2,000 people working for them.

7 My mum's in *education / finance*. She's an accountant at the hospital.

8 I know he's in *law / healthcare*. He's a solicitor, I think.

Decisions

1 Match the sentence halves.

1 Come on, Alice. Make up ☐

2 Can you be quiet? I find it difficult to make ☐

3 It's an important decision. I need to think long ☐

4 Don't worry. You can always change ☐

5 It's been ten minutes already. Have you come ☐

a and hard about it.

b your mind later if you want to.

c your mind. Do you want a sandwich or not?

d to a decision yet?

e a decision when people are talking.

Permission

1 Choose the correct option.

1 Do your parents *allow / let / make* you do whatever you want?
2 I'm not *allowed / let / made* to go out on a school night.
3 My parents *let / make / allow* me do my homework before I can play on the tablet.
4 Our teacher *makes / lets / allows* us put up our hand if we want to ask a question.
5 My mum won't *allow / let / make* me come to your party.
6 Are we really *allowed / let / made* to go in that abandoned house?

2 Complete the sentences with the missing words.

1 Are you _____ to stay up late?
2 Does your teacher _____ you use phones in class?
3 Do your parents _____ you do your homework before you can watch TV?
4 Are you _____ to do any housework by your parents?
5 Do your parents _____ you to get up late at the weekends?
6 Do your teachers _____ you eat in class?

3 Write your answers to the questions in Exercise 2.

SUMMING UP

1 Put the dialogue in order.

☐	JIM	I hope you're right. Anyway, I'm allowed to use their family car.
1	JIM	Have you heard the news? I've got a summer job.
☐	JIM	I'm actually quite scared. I don't really have much experience with kids.
☐	JIM	I don't think I'm allowed to use it when I'm not working.
☐	JIM	Childminding for children from the same family every day.
☐	LUCY	Wow. You're very brave.
☐	LUCY	You'll be fine. You're kind and lively. That's all kids want.
☐	LUCY	You never know. You should ask them. A friend with a car! This is going to be a good summer.
☐	LUCY	Cool! Where are you going to take me?
☐	LUCY	Congratulations. What is it?

D NEW THINGS
Reporting verbs

1 Match each verb with a sentence.

invite	☐
recommend	☐
refuse	☐
explain	*1*
agree	☐
demand	☐
persuade	☐
encourage	☐

1 To get to the station, you need to take the number 3 bus.
2 No, Bella, I won't take you to the party.
3 I want you to get out of my house, Ben. Now!
4 Would you like to go to the cinema, Jenny?
5 Come on, Jim. Come to the party with me. You will? Great!
6 You should enter the talent show. You're brilliant at singing, Lucy.
7 Read this book, Matt. You'll love it.
8 OK, Simon. I'll talk to your dad and see if I can change his mind.

2 Report the sentences in Exercise 1.

1 He *explained how to get to the station by bus.*
2 She _____
3 He _____
4 She _____
5 He _____
6 She _____
7 He _____
8 She _____

3 Complete with the reporting verbs in Exercise 1. There are three you won't use.

I can't believe I've ¹_____ to do a parachute jump with Tim. How did that happen? It all started when he ²_____ to me about this children's charity that he is involved with. I said it sounded interesting and he ³_____ me along to one of their meetings. So I went to see what it's all about. I didn't know they were organising a sponsored parachute jump. They asked me to get involved and of course I ⁴_____. I mean, I'm not mad. But they kept on trying to ⁵_____ me to do it and in the end I gave in and said 'yes'. And now I can't get out of it.

Negative adjectives

1 Rewrite the sentences using a negative adjective.

0 I'm not happy.
   I'm unhappy.

1 It's not true.
   _____

2 It's not a formal party.
   _____

3 They're not patient.
   _____

4 That wasn't responsible of you.
   _____

5 Buy it. It's not expensive.
   _____

6 They're not polite children.
   _____

7 I don't think that's possible.
   _____

Changes

1 Match the sentence halves.

1 If you're bored, why don't you take ☐
2 The children are all doing ☐
3 If children form ☐
4 If he doesn't change his ☐
5 Why's it so difficult to break ☐
6 I'm not going to make ☐
7 I'm finding French too hard. I might give ☐
8 Sometimes I struggle ☐

a any resolutions this new year.
b up having lessons.
c to understand maths. It can be so hard.
d bad habits?
e good habits when they're young, they'll never forget them.
f up a new hobby?
g ways, he's going to get into trouble one day.
h really well at their new school.

Regrets: *I wish … / If only …*

1 For each situation write two regrets: one about the present and one about the past.

0 I can't afford to buy my mum a birthday present.
   I wish I had more money.
   If only I hadn't spent all my money on clothes.

1 Sara refuses to speak to me.
   _____
   _____

2 I'm so tired I want to go to bed but I'm stuck here in my Science lesson.
   _____
   _____

3 All the popular boys are in the school football team.
   _____
   _____

4 I'm bored.
   _____
   _____

SUMMING UP

1 Complete the dialogue with the words/phrases in the list. There are four extra words/phrases.

encourage | struggle | wasn't | unhappy
am not | impossible | take up | gave up
demand | impolite | hadn't given it up | refuse

MARTHA   What's up, Ben? You look a bit [1]_____.

BEN   I'm OK. I'm just bored. I've got nothing to do.

MARTHA   Why don't you [2]_____ a new hobby? That will fill your time.

BEN   Like what?

MARTHA   Guitar lessons. You've always wanted to play the guitar better.

BEN   That's true. I wish I [3]_____ when I was a teenager. I'd be really good now.

MARTHA   Well, it's not too late to start again.

BEN   It is. It's [4]_____ for someone my age to start learning an instrument.

MARTHA   What! You're 23!

BEN   I know but I really [5]_____ with learning new things. I wish I [6]_____ that way but I am.

MARTHA   OK then – be bored.

BEN   What! That's not very nice.

MARTHA   Well I'm trying to [7]_____ you but you [8]_____ to listen. I give up.

BEN   I'm sorry, Martha. I'm just joking. And, you're right – it's never too late to start something new. In fact, I think I might just do that. Do you know any good teachers?

MARTHA   That's more like it. In fact I do … My brother! He's great.

GRAMMAR

Verb patterns: *to* + infinitive or gerund `SB page 14`

1 ★☆☆ Write the verbs in the correct columns according to what they are followed by (*to* + infinitive or gerund).

~~keep~~ | suggest | manage | promise | ask
decide | detest | don't mind | miss | want
can't stand | enjoy | offer | choose

to + infinitive	gerund
	keep

2 ★★☆ Circle the correct form of the verbs to complete the mini-dialogues.

1 **JANE** Did Simon manage *to finish / finishing* his essay last night?

 HARRY Yes, so he's promised *coming / to come* climbing with us this weekend.

 JANE Fantastic. My dad's offered *to give / giving* us a lift to the climbing club.

2 **KATE** I suggested *to take / taking* a picnic but they don't want *to carry / carrying* it.

 SAM I don't mind *to carry / carrying* it.

3 **ELIF** Now I live in the city, I miss *to go / going* for long walks in the countryside.

 JO Really? I can't stand *to walk / walking* in the countryside.

4 **ANNA** You're very good at the violin!

 ZOE No, I'm not. I really enjoy *to play / playing* and I keep *to practise / practising* but I'm not getting any better.

 ANNA Ask Tom *to help / helping* you. He's a brilliant musician.

5 **STEVE** You'll never guess what? Tim came climbing with us.

 ELLIE But Tim detests *to climb / climbing*!

3 ★★☆ Complete the text with the correct form of the verbs in brackets.

I enjoy ¹ _____ (climb) mountains, so last year, I decided ² _____ (climb) Ben Nevis in Scotland with a friend. We planned ³ _____ (go) to Scotland in August, and we arranged ⁴ _____ (stay) with a friend in Fort William for a few days. We started our climb at six am, and we hoped ⁵ _____ (get back) down the mountain by two pm. The weather was good, so we managed ⁶ _____ (reach) the summit in two hours. We never imagined ⁷ _____ (see) such a beautiful view from the summit. The next day, we felt like ⁸ _____ (climb) Ben Nevis again.

4 ★★★ Find five mistakes in the dialogue and correct them.

KATE I can't believe it. I managed climbing Devil's Rock this weekend.

MATT Did you? That's great.

KATE I've watched you climb it a couple of times but I never imagined to climb it myself. I'm hoping doing more climbing next weekend. I learnt descending the rock face using the rope. That was scary! What did you do at the weekend?

MATT I wanted coming climbing with you and the others but I had some homework to do.

5 ★★★ Complete the sentences so that they are true for you.

1 I enjoy _____

2 I started _____

3 I don't mind _____

4 I hate _____

5 I refuse _____

6 I love _____

Verbs + gerund and *to* + infinitive with different meanings SB page 15

6 ★☆☆ Match the sentences with their meanings.

1 I stopped to look at the view. ☐
2 I stopped looking at the view. ☐
3 He remembers buying a newspaper. ☐
4 Remember to buy a newspaper, Tom. ☐
5 He tried learning Chinese. ☐
6 He tried to learn Chinese. ☐
7 I'll never forget reading that article in the newspaper. ☐
8 I forgot to read that article in the newspaper. ☐

a I'll always remember that article I read in the newspaper.
b He knows he bought a newspaper.
c I didn't remember to read that article in the newspaper.
d He wasn't able to learn Chinese.
e I didn't look at the view any more.
f Don't forget to buy a newspaper.
g I stopped so I could look at the view.
h His goal was to impress his clients by speaking Chinese.

7 ★★☆ Complete the mini-dialogues with the correct form of the verbs in brackets.

1 A I forgot _____ (tell) you. We're going to London this weekend.
  B Lucky you!
2 A Did Helena finish her essay?
  B No, she didn't. She tried _____ (finish) it last night but she couldn't.
3 A I regret _____ (not leave) earlier on Saturday.
  B Yes, you missed the boat race.
4 A Do you still play the piano?
  B No, I stopped _____ (play) when I was nine.
5 A Do you remember _____ (lend) me JK Rowling's latest book?
  B Yes, I do. You haven't given it back yet.
6 A You left your guitar at Karen's house. Her mum rang me this morning.
  B Yes, I know. I stopped _____ (pick it up) on the way home just now.

8 ★★☆ Complete the sentences with the correct form of the verbs in the list.

eat | listen | tell | watch

1 I was revising for the History exam and then I stopped _____ to some music.
2 I listened to the first three songs and then I stopped _____ .
3 I remember _____ that film last year.
4 Remember _____ that film tonight. It's really good.
5 I've tried _____ more vegetables but I don't like them.
6 I tried _____ less but I still didn't lose any weight.
7 I regret _____ you that there aren't any more tickets for the concert.
8 I regret _____ Emma about the trip last weekend.

9 ★★★ Now write a true sentence for each of the situations. Think of …

1 something you regret doing or saying.

_____

2 something you remember doing or saying when you were in primary school.

_____

3 something you've tried doing.

_____

4 something you've stopped doing.

_____

5 something you forgot to do recently.

_____

GET IT RIGHT!

to or gerund after certain verbs

Learners often omit *to* or the gerund after certain verbs.

✓ We decided **to** go out for a meal.

✗ We decided ~~go~~ out for a meal.

Correct the errors in the sentences.

1 Jenny couldn't afford do the survival course.

_____

2 He started feel a bit awkward as no one was talking to him.

_____

3 Ethan suggested have an early night before the exam.

_____

4 I never promised help you with your homework!

_____

5 Do they practise to sing every evening?

_____

6 We wanted leave right away but we couldn't.

_____

VOCABULARY

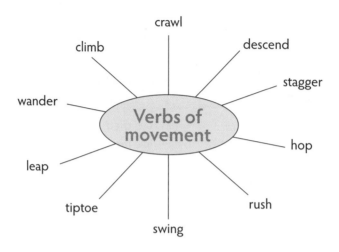

Verbs of movement

- crawl
- climb
- descend
- stagger
- wander
- hop
- leap
- rush
- tiptoe
- swing

Adjectives to describe uncomfortable feelings

puzzled
stuck
desperate

ashamed
guilty
awkward

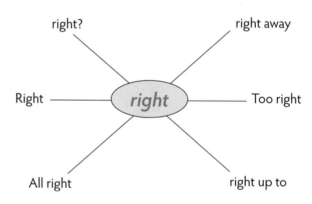

right

- right?
- right away
- Right
- Too right
- All right
- right up to

Key words in context

commercially	I don't think your product will be **commercially** successful. You won't have very many sales.
extreme	The weather conditions were **extreme**. It was very unusual to see such a snowstorm.
knot	He tied a **knot** at the end of the rope.
risky	It was **risky** to climb down the rock face without a safety rope but they had to do it.
shelter	It was snowing hard. We had to build a **shelter** to protect us from the snow and the cold.
slip	I **slipped** on the ice and fell over backwards.
stunt	That was a dangerous **stunt**. He jumped over three buses on a motorbike.
thrilled	I was **thrilled** when I won the race. My mum and dad were very happy too.
ultimate	Climbing Ben Nevis was the **ultimate** challenge for Jake. He had trained for months.

Verbs of movement SB page 14

1 ★☆☆ **Find ten verbs of movement.**

O	C	L	I	M	B	T	T	T	H	P
D	S	S	A	Y	N	I	E	C	A	H
N	W	C	A	T	B	P	L	E	T	R
E	I	W	R	R	K	T	L	A	G	E
C	N	S	E	A	L	O	P	W	L	G
S	G	M	E	E	W	E	S	O	E	G
E	H	R	U	S	H	L	I	N	H	A
D	W	A	N	D	E	R	T	D	E	T
B	R	E	A	T	H	L	E	G	R	S

2 ★★☆ **Complete the text about the race with the past tense of the verbs of movement in Exercise 1. There are two you won't use.**

Jake [0] *crawled* through the tunnel on his hands and knees. Then he held onto the rope and [1]_____ across the river. He [2]_____ very quietly past the house on the other side of the river. Then he quickly [3]_____ up the mountain. In thick fog, he slowly [4]_____ down the other side of the mountain. After that, he [5]_____ across the flat ground. He was in a hurry to finish now. Then suddenly, he fell and hurt his left leg, so he [6]_____ on his right leg to the finish line. Everybody cheered. He [7]_____ through the crowds of people and he shook hands with all his fans.

Adjectives to describe uncomfortable feelings SB page 16

3 ★★☆ **Read the situations. How would you feel? Choose one of the adjectives.**

1   You don't know the answer to the next question on the exam paper. You can't do the next question until you've completed this one.
    You are *stuck / puzzled*.

2   Last night you ate your brother's chocolate bar. He doesn't know yet.
    You feel *guilty / desperate*.

3   You are at a party. Everybody knows each other but you don't know anybody.
    You feel *awkward / puzzled*.

4   You put your house keys on the desk. Now they aren't there.
    You are *ashamed / puzzled*.

5   You shouted at one of your friends yesterday.
    You feel *ashamed / guilty* of yourself.

6   You are locked in a room in a castle. You have no phone and there is no food. Nobody knows you are there.
    You feel *desperate / stuck*.

4 ★★★ **Write a new situation for each feeling.**

1   (puzzled)
    _____

2   (stuck)
    _____

3   (desperate)
    _____

4   (ashamed)
    _____

5   (guilty)
    _____

6   (awkward)
    _____

WordWise SB page 19

right

5 ★★☆ **Complete the mini-dialogues with the phrases in the list.**

right | right away | Too right
right up to | All right | Right

1   A   Karen's just emailed me about the concert on Saturday. Do we want tickets?
    B   Of course we do.
    A   I'll email her back _____ then.

2   A   Did you guess who the thief was?
    B   No, I didn't know _____ the end of the book.

3   A   Did you remember to buy the tickets?
    B   I didn't buy them in the end. They were £50 a ticket. That's too expensive.
    A   _____ . I don't want to pay that much for a ticket either.

4   A   Sorry, I'll just answer the phone.
    B   Go ahead.
    [later]
    A   Sorry about that. It was James. _____ . What were we talking about?

5   A   Can I come with you and Sam to the match on Saturday?
    B   Yes, of course.
    A   You're setting off early, _____ ?
    B   Yes, we're leaving at 8 o'clock.

6   A   Can I borrow your ruler?
    B   _____ . But don't forget to give me it back.

READING

1 **REMEMBER AND CHECK** Answer these questions. Then check your answers on page 13 in the Student's Book.

1 Why did Simon and Joe decide to take the more dangerous route down the Siula Grande?

2 Why did the trip take longer than they had expected?

3 What did Joe break?

4 Why did Simon decide to leave his friend, Joe?

5 How long did it take Joe to descend the rest of the mountain?

6 Who saved Joe's life?

2 **Read the article quickly and answer the questions.**

1 Which body parts need to be very strong to free climb?

2 What is the importance of these numbers: 914, 19 and 27?

A Story of Teamwork and Perseverance

How do you climb a smooth rock face? In 2015, two young American climbers showed us how. Tommy Caldwell and Kevin Jorgeson became the first free climbers to climb the Dawn Wall of the El Capitan rock formation in California.

Free climbers don't use ropes when they climb. They only use their hands and feet. However, they do have ropes to hold them if they fall.

El Capitan is 914m high. That's almost 100m higher than the world's tallest building, the Burj Khalifa tower in Dubai, which is 163 floors high. The climb took Caldwell and Jorgeson 19 days. They ate, drank and slept in small tents hanging from the rock face. They even read books there! They brewed coffee on special hanging stoves. Every few days, a friend on the ground climbed up on a rope and brought them new supplies of food and water.

So how do you climb a smooth rock face? A lot of it relies on the strength of your fingertips. The climbers needed to stop and rest some days so that their fingertips could heal. To make their cuts heal quicker they used superglue and tape.

Unlike expeditions of a hundred years ago, people around the world could watch every moment of this climb as it happened. In their breaks, the climbers updated their social media accounts and spoke to journalists on the phone. A photographer and good friend, also hanging off the wall, captured every move on film and uploaded the photos on Instagram for people all around the world to see. 'Inspirational' – 'What a remarkable achievement! I'm awed.' – 'Awesome! Amazing! And a true friendship!' – 'What bravery and courage!' These are just some of the comments people tweeted as they watched the amazing climb.

A lot of the climbing was at night and they chose to climb in the middle of winter. Why was that? Well, fingertips sweat less in cooler temperatures and the rubber on shoes can grip better. They began their climb on the 27th December 2014 and they planned to live on the wall until they reached the top. They promised not to return to the ground during their climb.

Caldwell was the stronger and more experienced climber, and he was always ahead of Jorgeson. For ten days, Jorgeson continued to fall during his daily climbs. He knew that he was delaying his friend. But this climb was about teamwork and friendship. 'More than anything, I want to get to the top together,' said Caldwell on day 13. He couldn't imagine finishing without his friend. Finally on day 19 the two climbers made it to the top.

3 **Read the article again and mark the sentences T (true) or F (false).**

1 Caldwell and Jorgeson were the first free climbers to manage to climb the wall. ☐

2 El Capitan is in a national park in New Mexico. ☐

3 El Capitan is a few metres shorter than the world's tallest building. ☐

4 People all around the world were able to see pictures of the climb on social media. ☐

5 The climbers' shoes grip better in warmer temperatures. ☐

6 They started to climb the Dawn Wall in January 2015. ☐

7 The two climbers decided not to descend to the ground until they had successfully reached the top of the Dawn Wall. ☐

8 Caldwell wanted to finish the climb before his friend, Jorgeson. ☐

4 **Many people tweeted as they watched the amazing climb. What comment would you make?**

Pronunciation

Dipthongs: alternative spellings
Go to page 118.

DEVELOPING WRITING

A travel advertisement: review for an adventure holiday

1 Read Miriam's review. What do you notice about the style of writing?

a It is formal. ☐

b It is informal. ☐

2 What does Miriam use in her review?

a She uses some questions. ☐

b She uses very long sentences. ☐

My Climb to Confidence

What's 4,167 metres high, in Morocco and a challenge to climb? Mount Toubkal of course! Mount Toubkal is North Africa's highest mountain. And guess what? I managed to climb it this autumn. Yes, I actually climbed to the summit of a mountain.

The climb was a fantastic experience. The trekking was tough though, especially on the final day. We walked for twelve hours, and on the other three days we walked for eight or nine hours. I was exhausted when we finally reached the camp each evening. It was a four-day trek and we spent three icy cold nights camping. I went with my mum and dad and my older brother, who's nineteen. The climb was challenging for all of us. Each day, we stopped to have a picnic lunch, and the views were spectacular. I really regret not taking a camera. The rest of the holiday was fun too, but the climb up Mount Toubkal was the highlight for me. I think the whole trip was character building and I definitely feel more confident now I've done it.

Any tips? Yes. Remember to take a hat. The sun is fierce. Don't forget to take a water bottle with you and some water purification tablets. Prepare for a challenging walk.

3 Answer the questions.

1 How does Miriam describe Mount Toubkal?
_____

2 How did Miriam feel when she reached the camp each evening?
_____

3 Who did Miriam go with?
_____

4 How did Miriam feel after the trip?
_____

5 What tips does Miriam give?
_____

4 Read the review again and find the adjectives. What do they describe? Write the nouns/ pronouns. Then look in a thesaurus and find another adjective you could use instead.

Adjective	Noun	My new choice of adjective
1 tough	*trekking*	
2 exhausted		
3 icy cold		
4 challenging		
5 spectacular		
6 fierce		

5 Write a review for an adventure holiday. It can be for a holiday you have been on or a made up holiday. Write 200–250 words.

CHECKLIST

☐ Use informal language

☐ Include interesting adjectives

☐ Use verbs of movement

☐ Include an introductory paragraph, main body, conclusion and travel tips

LISTENING

1 🔊04 Read the sentences below. Then listen and write the numbers of the dialogues, 1, 2 or 3 in the boxes.

1 They are in the middle of a challenge. One of them wants to give up. ☐

2 They have climbed a high mountain and they want a new challenge. ☐

3 They watch a video about people running, climbing, jumping and swinging over walls and buildings. ☐

2 🔊04 Listen again and complete the sentences with one word.

1 Sammy wants James to come and watch a _____

2 Parkour started in _____ .

3 Chris can't continue because he can't crawl through the _____ .

4 The weather's very bad. It's just started to _____ .

5 Jake enjoys going to the climbing club because everyone is very _____ .

6 The climb up Ben Nevis was a _____ for Jake.

DIALOGUE

1 Complete these parts of the dialogues with the phrases in the list.

Of course you can | that's too easy | I bet you |
I think you're probably right | I'll never manage to |
I bet you | I challenge you | No problem

1 SAMMY   Wow! Did you see that?
_____ can't do that.

   JAMES   _____ can.

   SAMMY   All right. _____ to jump onto the kitchen table.

   JAMES   But _____ .

   SAMMY   Yes, easy and safe. You need proper training to do Parkour.

2 CHRIS   You go on ahead, Susie.
_____ crawl through that tunnel.

   SUSIE   _____ , Chris. Come on. Keep going. You're doing really well. I bet you can crawl through that tunnel faster than I can.

3 JAKE   It was a challenge but I'm glad I've done it.

   LOUISE   Same here. What's our next challenge? I bet we can climb Mount Everest one day.

   JAKE   _____ . It won't be for a few years though. I don't think we're ready for that yet.

   LOUISE   _____ . We need a bit more practice before we take on that challenge. Now, where were we? … I know. You were showing me how to do that knot.

PHRASES FOR FLUENCY SB page 19

1 Match the two halves of the phrases.

1 Same   ☐   a a shout
2 Something ☐   b what?
3 Give me   ☐   c deal
4 You know   ☐   d were we?
5 Where   ☐   e here
6 It's a   ☐   f or other

2 Complete the dialogues with phrases from Exercise 1.

1 A Come along to the indoor climbing club and I'll teach you. I'm a trainer there.

   B _____ When do I start?

2 A Dinner's not ready yet.

   B OK. _____ when it's ready.

3 A Rob's going on an adventure holiday this September. It's a trek across the desert in Jordan.

   B I know. I thought he was crazy at first. But _____ Now I think I want to go with him. It's a real challenge.

4 A Sorry about that, Matt. I had to answer a call. Now, _____

   B You were just showing me the route for Saturday's trek.

   A Ah, yes.

5 A I'm sorry I haven't called you this week. I've had a lot of things to do.

   B _____ I've been really busy with the band.

6 A Have you seen Kate recently?

   B No. She's at football training or tennis club or _____

Reading and Use of English Part 4

1 For questions 1–5, complete the second sentence so that it has a similar meaning to the first sentence, using the word given. Do not change the word given. You must use between two and five words, including the word given. Here is an example (0).

Example:

0   I moved here five years ago.
   FOR
   I _'ve lived here for five_ years.

1   I would rather not see that film.
   PREFER
   I _____ that film.

2   I won't leave him there alone.
   REFUSE
   I _____ there alone.

3   I can't afford to buy this laptop.
   ENOUGH
   I _____ money to buy this laptop.

4   She wasn't able to complete her homework last night.
   MANAGE
   She _____ her homework last night.

5   I remember my first swimming lesson.
   FORGET
   I _____ first swimming lesson.

Exam guide: key word transformation

In this part of the exam, there are six questions. Each has a complete sentence and a second gapped sentence. You must complete the second sentence with two to five words so that it means the same as the first sentence. There is a key word which you must include.

- Remember contractions count as two words.
- You should always give every question a try. It's possible to get a point for one correct word.
- Train yourself to think of different ways of saying things.

2 For questions 1–6, complete the second sentence so that it has a similar meaning to the first sentence, using the word given. Do not change the word given. You must use between two and five words, including the word given. Here is an example (0).

Example:

0   My mum didn't let me go to the cinema last night.
   ALLOW
   My mum _didn't allow me to_ go to the cinema last night.

1   It's been months since I last went swimming.
   BEEN
   I _____ several months.

2   We haven't got enough time to go and see the art exhibition.
   TOO
   It's _____ and see the art exhibition.

3   I couldn't see the play last night.
   ABLE TO
   I _____ the play last night.

4   Nobody has managed to climb that rock face yet.
   SUCCEEDED
   Nobody _____ that rock face yet.

5   I stopped so I could buy a newspaper.
   TO
   I _____ a newspaper.

6   I'd like to have a bath.
   FEEL
   I _____ a bath.

2 GOING PLACES

GRAMMAR

Relative clauses (review) SB page 22

1 ★★☆ **Complete the gaps with *who, which* or *that* and put D (defining) or ND (non-defining).**

0   People ___who___ move to a big city can find it hard to meet people. | D |

1   My sister Jane, _____ lives in New York, has made a lot of friends there. | |

2   The café, _____ opened near the university, is a good place to meet people. | |

3   Paul, _____ has just moved in next door to me, has four sisters. | |

4   It's not always easy to meet people _____ like the same things as you. | |

5   Of the six flats, the one _____ Sally shares with four friends is the smallest. | |

2 ★★☆ **Find and correct the mistakes in each sentence.**

0   I'm very proud of my mother who works for a local charity.
    I'm very proud of my mother, who works for a local charity.

1   This is a photograph who I took in Italy.

2   The boy which bought my bike lives in this street.

3   My mother who is a doctor often has to work at weekends.

4   I've got a new phone who is far better than my old one.

5   The player, who scored the winning goal in the 2014 World Cup final, was Mario Götze.

6   I don't really like people, who talk a lot.

which to refer to a whole clause SB page 22

3 ★☆☆ **Write sentences from the prompts, using *which*.**

0   Some people / listen / to very loud music / can / damage / their ears
    Some people listen to very loud music, which can damage their ears.

1   My father / walks / to work / is / good / for his health

2   My grandfather / has / three large dogs / means / he / gets / plenty of exercise

3   Some blind people / have / guide dogs / gives / them more independence

4   My sister / spends / hours / working / on the computer / sometimes / gives / her / a headache

4 ★★☆ **Find pairs of ideas. Then write sentences using *which*. Make any other necessary changes.**

0   ~~bus to school / cost £2.50~~
1   I like / watch films at home
2   friend / going / live in Colombia
3   mother's car / stolen last week
4   famous band / play in our town next week

a   be / big change in lifestyle
b   ~~be / very expensive for me~~
c   not happen / very often
d   mean / take bus to work
e   be / cheaper / go / cinema

0   *The bus to school costs £2.50, which is very expensive for me.*

1   _____

2   _____

3   _____

4   _____

Omitting relative pronouns and reduced relative clauses SB page 25

5 ★☆☆ **Complete the gaps with that / which / who or – if the pronoun is not necessary.**

1 Patrick paid back the money _____ he owed me last week.

2 I know a lot of people _____ have eaten at that restaurant.

3 There are a few things _____ I want to keep with me.

4 This is the book _____ Mimi gave me for my birthday.

5 These aren't the photos _____ were in the newspaper.

6 I'm the sort of person _____ likes to spend time alone.

6 ★★☆ **Complete the dialogue with who / which / that or – if the pronoun is not necessary.**

JANET Greg, you've moved a lot. What are the things [1]_____ you think are important about moving?

GREG Yes, well, I think the thing [2]_____ is most important is to be optimistic about the move. Of course there are things [3]_____ you'll miss, but think of all the exciting things there will be. New places, new people!

JANET But what about my friends? This is the only place [4]_____ I've ever lived in!

GREG You can keep in touch with the people [5]_____ are your most important friends. And you can visit – you're going to live in Ireland, right? Not on the moon!

JANET I know, but you need to take a train and then the ferry, [6]_____ makes it complicated and expensive. And what if I don't make new friends?

GREG Look, don't worry! You're an outgoing person [7]_____ makes friends quickly – you'll be OK. But you know, one thing [8]_____ I like to do before I move is make a scrapbook [9]_____ will remind me of the place and the people. I put photos, names, birthdays and email addresses in it, [10]_____ helps me to keep in touch with the friends [11]_____ I made.

JANET That's a great idea! Thanks, Greg.

7 ★★☆ **Join the sentences to make one sentence.**

0 Catarina is an Italian student. She is studying English in London.
  Catarina is an Italian student studying English in London.

1 Walter fell and hurt himself. He was painting a wall.
  _____

2 We gave a lift to two students. They were trying to get to London.
  _____

3 I met a French guy on the train. He was going to the same place as me.
  _____

4 A scientist accidentally discovered Post-It notes. He was trying to invent a strong glue.
  _____

5 The crew of the ship found a man. He was hiding in the lifeboat.
  _____

GET IT RIGHT! ◉

which and who

A common error for learners is to use *which* instead of *who* or vice versa in relative clauses.

✓ *I met some friendly people **who** became friends of mine.*

✗ *I met some friendly people ~~which~~ became friends of mine.*

Complete the sentences with *which* or *who*.

1 Please let me know _____ is the most direct way to the conference.

2 Most of the immigrants _____ moved to the village found work.

3 The motorists _____ use this road are kindly asked to drive more slowly.

4 There are a lot of people moving to this area, _____ means there will be fewer parking places.

5 Sam had a year out in Italy, _____ is a beautiful country.

6 Lucy turned out to be someone _____ you can rely on.

7 The Aborigines, _____ have been living there for 40,000 years, have few possessions.

8 The boat _____ the refugees were sailing on arrived safely in the port.

VOCABULARY

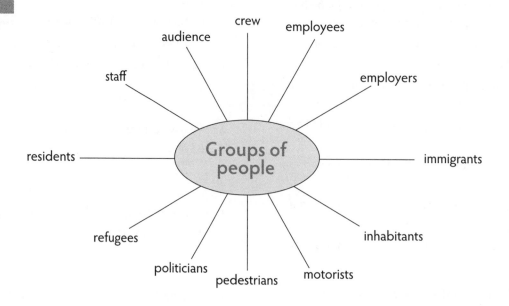

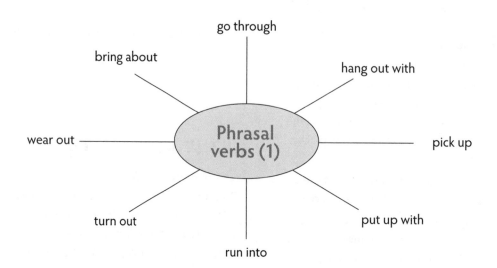

Key words in context

abroad	I don't live in my own country anymore – I live **abroad**.
compassion	She's had a very bad time recently – we need to show her some **compassion**.
courage	I've never sung in front of other people – I don't have the **courage**.
desperately	They've got no money at all – they're **desperately** poor.
homesickness	After two months away from home, my **homesickness** started to get better.
invaluable	I would never have succeeded without your help – it was **invaluable**.
mayor	In our city, we choose a new **mayor** every four years.
overall	We had a few days of rain, but mostly it was sunny, so **overall** the summer's been good.
praise	He told the truth and people **praised** him for his honesty.
renovate	My house is old now, so I'm going to **renovate** it.
severe	Sometimes the temperature is -25° – the winter can be really **severe**.
shortage	It hasn't rained for six months, so now we've got a water **shortage**.

Groups of people SB page 22

1 ★★☆ Complete the crossword.

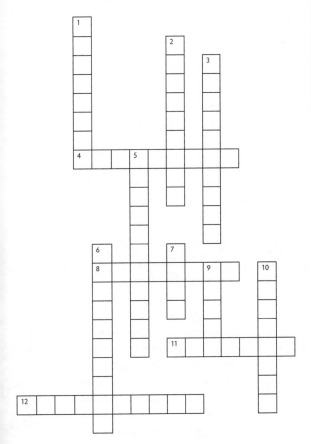

1 The factory is the town's biggest …

2 It's a really big company – there are more than a thousand … there.

3 You can't drive here – this is a … zone.

4 Big, noisy lorries use this street, and some … are unhappy about it.

5 It's a huge city – there are about twelve million … here.

6 There is a large population of North African … in our town.

7 The plane was carrying 90 passengers and seven … members.

8 The accident was caused by a … who was driving too fast.

9 There are more than 30 teachers on the … of the school.

10 A lot of people in the … didn't like the film, and started to leave.

11 She escaped from her country and now she's a …

12 She's an important … and hopes to become the leader of her party soon.

Pronunciation
Phrasal verb stress
Go to page 118. 🔊

2 ★★☆ Which people might say these things? (There may be more than one possibility.)

1 _Cyclists – they're terrible, I can't stand them._

2 _The boss is OK but she makes us work really hard too!_

3 _I promise that we will make this country better._

4 _It isn't always easy to make a new start in another country._

5 _Speak up! We can't hear you here at the back._

6 _We really love living here – it's great._

Phrasal verbs (1) SB page 24

3 ★☆☆ Circle the correct options.

1 I thought the exam would be difficult, but it _turned out / brought about_ to be easy.

2 He's horrible – why do you _hang out with / run into_ him?

3 The neighbours are so noisy – I can't _go through / put up with_ it any more.

4 We complained so much that we _brought about / picked up_ some changes.

5 I don't really speak Japanese – I just _picked up / put up with_ some phrases.

6 Isn't it funny when you _run into / hang out with_ someone you haven't seen for ages?

7 I worked really hard on Monday – I was _turned out / worn out._

8 Don't worry – it's just a bad time I'm _wearing out / going through._

4 ★★☆ Complete each sentence with one or two words.

1 Yesterday I ran _____ an old friend of my mother's.

2 They walk so quickly that they wear me _____ !

3 Everyone said it was going to rain, but it turned _____ to be a lovely day.

4 I'm going to hang _____ my friends this afternoon.

5 Be nice to her – she's going _____ a bad time right now.

6 He's never had French lessons – he just picked it _____ in France.

7 We hope these changes will bring _____ some better results.

8 You're horrible! I don't know why I put _____ you!

READING

1 REMEMBER AND CHECK Match the phrases from columns A, B and C. Then check your answers in the text on page 21 of the Student's Book.

A	B	C
1 Many young people	started an organisation	to house the refugees.
2 Domenico Lucano	went and visited Riace	because there weren't enough jobs.
3 Lucano	had to work	called Città Futura.
4 The refugees	saw some people on the beach	to get ideas for their towns and cities.
5 Lucano	used empty buildings	who had escaped their own country.
6 The male refugees	which meant that	so they could be rented to tourists.
7 There are more children,	left Riace	to earn their food and accommodation.
8 Other politicians	renovated houses	the school could reopen.

2 Read the blog. How does the writer usually feel about getting lost? How did she feel at the end of this story?

The joys of getting lost

Most of us like to know where we are and where we're going. It can feel strange to be lost – sometimes very uncomfortable, too. The words 'being lost' make us think of a dark wood, or a dark city street: threatening and scary. But that's not always the case.

When I was about twelve, we were on holiday in Venice. My dad's a really keen photographer and he said that he was going to get up the following morning at 5 o'clock and go out to take photos as the sun came up. Mum wasn't interested, but I said I'd go with him. (Of course, that was only because he promised I could have the biggest ever bowl of Italian ice cream if I did! Why else would I get up at 5 in the morning?!)

So at 5 am we left the hotel and started walking. There was almost no one in the streets, which is pretty rare in Venice.

As the sun began to come up, Dad started taking photographs and I just looked around. Every time he walked off, I followed him, down small streets and over little bridges.

After about an hour and a half, I turned to him. 'Dad,' I asked, 'where are we?' He looked at me and said, 'You know, I have no idea.' I immediately felt a bit scared, but Dad just smiled and laughed. 'We're lost!' he said. I told him to get out his map or phone. He looked at me. 'Map? Phone? I only brought the camera. Come on, let's get more lost!' And he laughed again.

His laughter relaxed me and made me feel safe. We started to walk again. People were appearing on the streets – shops and cafés began to open, and as the sun came up the narrow streets started to fill with light, to Dad's delight.

I began to forget that we were lost, and just started watching and taking in everything that was happening around me. We stopped and had a sandwich for breakfast – Dad's terrible Italian was just enough for us to get what we wanted, even in a place away from the tourist track.

Finally, after about four hours of wandering around, Dad said: 'Hey! This is our street!' And we were back. Mum was in the breakfast room of the hotel when we came in. 'Where have you been?' she asked, anxiously. 'We got lost!' I said with a huge grin.

These days we have so many things to stop us from getting lost – maps, GPS, apps on our phones, and so on. But Dad showed me that being lost can sometimes simply be something to enjoy.

3 Read the blog again. Mark the sentences T (true), F (false) or DS (doesn't say).

1 When people think of 'being lost', they sometimes feel scared. ☐
2 The writer's father is a professional photographer. ☐
3 The streets in Venice are often empty. ☐
4 The writer's father never took his phone with him when he took photographs. ☐
5 The writer's father spoke good Italian. ☐
6 They had breakfast in a place where tourists often went. ☐
7 The writer's mother was worried about them. ☐
8 The writer now gets lost quite often, in order to have adventures. ☐

4 Write a short paragraph (50–80 words) to say how you feel about getting lost. Give an example of a time it happened to you.

DEVELOPING WRITING

Writing a letter to a friend

1 Read Marcos's letter to Jodie.

  1 Where is he?

  2 What difficulties does he talk about?

Hi Jodie,

How's everything with you in England? ¹<u>Sorry</u> I haven't written before but there's just been so much to do since I left Brazil to come here.

   And now here I am in Vancouver, on my year exchange! You know that I'm staying with a family here, right? They're the Johnsons, who live in an area called Oakridge: it's a few kilometres from the city centre but there are buses and a train, so ²<u>easy to</u> get there. The Johnsons are very friendly and they've helped me settle in. They haven't got any kids but I've made some friends my age round here, and I go to the language course three mornings a week and I've got friends there too.

   Talking of language – well, that's been the tricky thing, especially listening. People don't talk like in the books at school! I mean, ³<u>no problem</u> when I'm talking to one person, but in a big group, it can be hard to follow the conversation. Still, it's getting easier!

   Otherwise, ⁴<u>all good</u>. I thought a lot of things would be very different here, but they aren't. One thing, though, is you have to remember to leave a tip in restaurants. ⁵<u>Not like</u> in Brazil, where the tip's always added to the bill. And when you buy something, you have to remember that they add tax at the check-out so you always pay more than what's on the label!

   OK, ⁶<u>got</u> to go. Write and tell me how you are.

Marcos

2 In each of the underlined parts of the letter, Marcos left something out before the underlined word(s). Match these phrases to the underlined parts 1–6.

  a there's ☐   b I'm ☐   c it's ☐   d It's ☐   e I've ☐   f it's ☐

Writing tip

- We often leave certain words out in informal speaking and writing (it's called *ellipsis*). It is usually the subject and the auxiliary verb that are left out, for example:
Did you have a nice weekend? becomes *Have a nice weekend?* (leaving out the subject 'you' and the auxiliary 'did')

3 What could be left out from these sentences? Rewrite the sentences.

  0 It's good to see you.
    Good to see you.

  1 There are no worries, we can do this easily.

  2 Are you having a good time?

  3 Do you see what I mean?

4 Imagine that you are doing an exchange programme in an English-speaking country. Write a letter to a friend about your experience. Write 200–250 words.

Include:
- which country you are in
- who you are staying with
- what difficulties you've had with language
- any cultural differences you've had to adjust to.

CHECKLIST ✔

  ☐ Use a style of an informal letter
  ☐ Use at least two examples of ellipsis
  ☐ Mention language and cultural difference
  ☐ Write 200–250 words

LISTENING

1 🔊 06 **Listen to two conversations. Complete each sentence with between 1 and 3 words.**

CONVERSATION 1

1 Jill has won a _____ a magazine.

2 The prize is a _____ day trip to South Africa.

3 She won't have to _____ on the trip.

4 Max wants to know how many people _____ is for.

CONVERSATION 2

5 Monika and Graham are looking at _____ comic books.

6 Monika's grandfather collects _____ .

7 He started his collection when he was _____ as a young man.

8 _____ the money in his collection is old.

2 🔊 06 **Listen again. Complete these parts of the conversations with 1 or 2 words.**

CONVERSATION 1

JILL Well, in ¹_____, I entered it. I kind of thought I knew lots of the answers, most of them in fact. And so I thought 'OK, why not?'

MAX And …? Hold on, you're not telling me …

JILL Yes. I won! I heard today. The magazine phoned me up and told me I'd won.

MAX That's ²_____! Wow. Well done. So – you've got a free trip to South Africa?

JILL That's right. I can ³_____ it myself.

CONVERSATION 2

GRAHAM Do you collect anything, Monika?

MONIKA No – but my grandfather's got ⁴_____ collection of money from all over the world. I think he's got coins and notes from ⁵_____ a hundred different countries.

GRAHAM That's ⁶_____ collection!

DIALOGUE

1 **Put the dialogues in order.**

1

☐ A Go on – surprise me.

[1] A I hear you're going to Scotland for the weekend.

☐ A That's incredible.

☐ B Well, I got a return ticket for £57.50.

☐ B I know. It's amazing, isn't it? I could hardly believe it myself.

☐ B Yes, by train. I bought a really cheap ticket online last night. You'll never believe what I paid.

2

☐ A Pretty interesting, I thought. You know, they move around with camels, and they can travel up to sixty kilometres a day.

☐ A Did you see the documentary last night about the Tuareg?

☐ A I know. And in that kind of heat. It's almost unbelievable.

☐ B No, I missed it. Was it any good?

☐ B I'm not sure I'd want to do it, I have to say.

☐ B Wow. That's quite a distance.

3

☐ A In Alaska. And it's winter there. He wrote me an email – he said that sometimes, it's -25 degrees.

☐ A My friend Pete's gone travelling around the world.

☐ A I know. How do people survive in temperatures like that?

☐ B Really? I knew it got cold there, but not that cold!

☐ B I've got a better question. Why on earth did Pete choose to go somewhere so cold!?

☐ B Oh, right. So where is he now?

2 **Write two dialogues of six lines each. Choose from these situations. Look back at Exercise 1 to help you.**

1 Two friends are talking. One of them watched a football match. A player scored five goals.

2 Two friends are talking. One of them did an online quiz and got 49/50.

3 Two friends are talking. One of them has a new friend who is 2.12 metres tall.

4 Two friends are talking. One of them is saving to buy a musical instrument. It's very expensive.

Writing part 2: an article

Exam guide: writing an article

In part 2 of the writing exam you are asked to write a text from a choice of text types in about 140–190 words. This will sometimes be an article, for example, for a school magazine or a teen website.

Remember that the article is for a magazine or website – it's for entertainment, rather than for information. So, try to make your writing lively and interesting. Ways you can do this include:

- using direct (rhetorical) questions
- using lots of adjectives and adverbs
- not making the sentences too long and complicated

Remember that in the actual exam your work is assessed on its:

- content (have you done what you're asked to do?)
- language (is your grammar, vocabulary and spelling generally good even if there are some mistakes?)
- organisation (does your writing follow a clear, logical pattern?)
- communication (is your writing in an appropriate style – not too formal or informal?)

Manuela wrote an article after she saw this task:

THE BEST PLACE I'VE EVER VISITED

What's the best place you've ever visited?

When did you go? Who with? What did you like so much about it?

Write and tell us.
Write about 140–190 words.

We'll publish the best articles on our website! And there are prizes for the winners!

1 **Read Manuela's article and answer the questions.**

1 Does she do everything that the task asks her to do?

_____

2 Find and circle:
a adjectives that she uses
b three 'questions' that she uses

The best place I've ever visited? It has to be Disney World, in Florida. We live in Mexico City and a trip to the USA had always been my dream. On my eleventh birthday, my parents gave me a white envelope instead of the usual present. And can you <u>guess what</u> it was? Of course – our plane tickets to spend six nights in Disney World. <u>I was just so</u> excited!

We flew about five weeks later. <u>I can still remember</u> so many things about that fantastic trip. We stayed in a resort in the Epcot Centre, and every day we went to see something different. I guess my real favourite was the Wild Africa Trek – three hours of walking and seeing wild animals – it was incredible. <u>And then there were</u> the rides, of course – we all got in a raft one afternoon and did some white-water rafting, that was scary but fun, we got drenched!

So we had five days of fun, sun, great food, ice cream, rides – what's not to like? <u>I can hardly wait to</u> go back!

2 **Look at the underlined phrases in the article. They are phrases that you could use in this kind of article writing. Can you find at least one other phrase you think you could use?**

3 **Write an article of your own. You can choose the task that Manuela did, or the one below.**

NOMADIC PEOPLE I'D LIKE TO KNOW

There are many nomadic people in the world – e.g. the Inuit and the Tuareg.
If you could meet and spend some time with a nomadic tribe, which one would it be and why?
Write and tell us. Write about 140–190 words.
We'll publish the best articles on our website!
And there are prizes for the winners!

CONSOLIDATION

LISTENING

1 🔊07 Listen to Amelia talking about her year in Indonesia. Put the things below in the order she mentions them. There are two she doesn't mention.

☐	the food	☐	the language
☐	her school	☐	transport
☐	the weather	☐	the people

2 🔊07 Listen again and mark the sentences T (true) or F (false).

1 Amelia's dad was only going to spend half a year there. ☐

2 The weather was always hot and dry. ☐

3 Amelia's lost contact with most of her Indonesian friends. ☐

4 She used to buy nasi goreng from a shop. ☐

5 Amelia describes a bejak journey as being a bit dangerous but exciting too. ☐

GRAMMAR

3 Choose the correct option.

1 I don't mind *to help* / *helping* you with your homework.

2 But, Dad, you promised *to take* / *taking* me to the cinema tonight!

3 I feel like *to eat* / *eating* some chocolate. I don't suppose you've got any?

4 Can I suggest *to take* / *taking* a break and finishing this later?

5 I really regret *to tell* / *telling* Paul all those things.

6 I bumped into Joshua on the high street and we stopped *to have* / *having* a chat.

7 I forgot *to post* / *posting* this letter again.

8 I don't remember *to invite* / *inviting* Ian to my party. Why's he here?

4 Join the sentences to make one sentence.

1 My sister spends all day on her phone. I find this very annoying.

_____

2 My favourite town is Brighton. It's on the south coast.

_____

3 I watched the film last night. I thought it was really boring.

_____

4 My best friend is Al. He was born on the same day as me.

_____

VOCABULARY

5 Match the sentence halves.

1 I don't know how you put up ☐

2 I'm ashamed of what I said and ☐

3 Housework really wears me ☐

4 I'm a bit stuck and ☐

5 I wasn't in Spain long and I only picked ☐

6 I felt a bit awkward and ☐

7 It was a terrible thing to go ☐

8 I can tell that he's guilty ☐

a out and makes me feel tired.

b through and she doesn't like talking about it.

c didn't know what to say.

d by the look on his face.

e could use some help.

f with all his terrible jokes.

g I want to say sorry.

h up a few words of the language.

6 Complete each word.

1 We had to c_____ on our hands and knees.

2 The r_____ are really unhappy about the plans to open a new nightclub in the area.

3 The c_____ made sure all the passengers were safely off the ship before they left.

4 They w_____ around the city for hours. They had no idea where they were going.

5 She t_____ quietly up the stairs.

6 The a_____ hated his performance and he was booed off stage.

7 The company has more than 1,000 e_____.

8 He grabbed the rope and s_____ across the river.

DIALOGUE

7 **Complete the dialogue with the phrases in the list. There are two you won't use.**

You know what? | You'll never manage to do it | It's a deal | That's too easy
Same here | Of course I can | I bet you can't | Give me a shout

DAN You can't go for more than an hour without checking your phone.

ANA ¹_____.

DAN No you can't. I mean we've only been in the restaurant 20 minutes and you've already checked it twice.

ANA Well, I'm expecting an important message.

DAN Really? ²_____ I don't think you could survive without your phone. Not even for five minutes. In fact, ³_____ spend the rest of the meal without your phone.

ANA Don't be silly. ⁴_____.

DAN Is it? OK, if you don't look at your phone until we finish eating, I'll pay for dinner.

ANA ⁵_____. I hope you've got a lot of money with you.

DAN I haven't but that's no problem. ⁶_____.

ANA OK, let's see.

READING

8 **Read the article and answer the questions.**

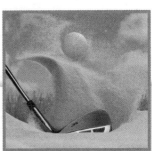

You would expect extreme sportspeople to be equipped with survival techniques. A mountaineer needs to be ready for a rapid descent in bad weather and a deep-sea diver needs to know what to do should they ever come face to face with a great white shark, for example. Even more everyday sportspeople need to know a few basic procedures and more than one football player's life has been saved by the actions of a quick-thinking team mate. But if there's one sport you would expect to be pretty safe, then it's golf. Apart from a few sand bunkers and maybe a pond or two, golf courses are hardly the most dangerous of places. Indeed, golf courses are often set in some of the most beautiful countryside there is. What could possibly go wrong there? In fact the only people who might be in danger are the spectators who run the risk of a golf ball landing on their head from time to time.

Swedish golfer Daniela Holmqvist might have a thing or two to say about this. She was in Australia playing in a tournament when she felt a nasty bite on her lower leg. When she looked she saw a small black spider on her ankle. She immediately brushed it away but the pain was getting stronger and stronger. She quickly called for help and was told that she had been bitten by a black widow spider,

one of the most poisonous creatures in the world. In fact, one bite can kill an adult in less than an hour. The local people were very concerned and immediately called for medical help. But Daniela knew she could not afford to wait for it. She knew she had to do something there and then as her leg had already started to swell.

From out of her pocket she pulled a tee, the plastic object that a golfer uses to place the ball on at the start of each hole. Using the sharp end of the tee, she made a hole in her leg and squeezed the poison out from inside. It came flowing out in a clear liquid. Despite the pain she kept applying pressure until all the fluid had been removed. Doctors were soon on the scene and helped bandage Daniela up. You might have thought that after a brush with death like this, you would want to go home and rest for a while. Not Daniela. Instead of taking any time off to recover, Daniela insisted on finishing the remaining 14 holes to complete her game.

1 What dangers might a mountaineer or a deep-sea diver encounter? _____

2 What dangers might a golfer encounter? _____

3 What danger did Daniela Holmqvist encounter?

_____

4 How did she react at first? _____

5 What did she do to survive the danger? _____

6 What did she do once the danger was over? _____

WRITING

9 **Think of a dangerous situation and write a paragraph about how you would respond. Write about 180 words.**

Include:
● what the situation was
● what you did
● how you felt afterwards

3 | THE NEXT GENERATION

GRAMMAR

Quantifiers SB page 32

1 ★☆☆ **Put the sentences in order (1–4) according to amount, 1 being the most.**

1

a She's got loads of cousins. [1]

b She's got a few cousins. [ ]

c She's got several cousins. [ ]

d She's got hardly any cousins. [ ]

2

a A small number of the children at our school go on to university. [ ]

b None of the children at our school go on to university. [ ]

c All of the children at our school go on to university. [ ]

d The vast majority of children at our school go on to university. [ ]

3

a Mum hardly spends any time at home. [ ]

b Mum spends plenty of time at home. [ ]

c Mum doesn't spend much time at home. [ ]

d Mum spends all her time at home. [ ]

2 ★★☆ **Complete the text with the words in the list.**

loads | number | plenty | most | majority
deal | few | almost | hardly | all of | several

I love the street where we live. There are ⁰ *loads* of houses and the vast ¹_____ have families living in them. That means there are always ²_____ of children to play with. There are ³_____ kids from my class at school and ⁴_____ us love football so ⁵_____ days you'll find us playing football in the park at the end of the street. The park is great and I spend ⁶_____ all of my time there. Of course, there are a small ⁷_____ of mean kids who hang out there but they don't usually bother us. At the other end of the road there are a ⁸_____ shops where I spend a good ⁹_____ of my pocket money on sweets. By Friday evening I've got ¹⁰_____ any pocket money left!

3 ★★☆ **Circle the correct option.**

1 My cousin's crazy about cars. He's got *loads of / hardly any / a few* books on them.

2 There's no need to hurry. We've got *several / plenty / the vast majority* of time.

3 *Hardly any / Several / Good deal* of the public trust politicians.

4 Let Phil pay. He's got *most / loads / all* of money.

5 The *vast majority / good deal / most* of children at our school speak two languages.

6 *All / A few / Several* of my cousins went to university so of course, Mum and Dad expect me to go too.

4 ★★★ **Choose quantifiers and complete the sentences so they are true for you.**

1 I spend _____ my time _____

2 _____ my friends _____

3 _____ the teachers at my school _____

4 _____ the children at my school _____

5 I spend _____ my money _____

6 I find _____ the subjects at school _____

so and *such* (review) SB page 35

5 ★★☆ **Rewrite the sentences using the word(s) in brackets.**

0 This is such a difficult question. (so)
   This question is so difficult.

1 It's such a hot day today. (so)
   _____

2 My uncle's so rich. (such / man)
   _____

3 Dawn's got so many problems. (such / a lot of)
   _____

4 I ate so much. (such)
   _____

6 ★★★ **Write continuations for the sentences in Exercise 5.**

0 *This question is so difficult that I've no idea what the answer is.*

too and *(not)* enough SB page 35

7 ★★☆ **Complete the sentence for each picture. Use *too* or *(not)* enough. Sometimes there is more than one possible answer.**

0 Sorry, *you're not old enough. / you're too young.*

1 Forget it, _____

_____

Let's come back later.

2 I can't do it, _____

_____

3 Do you know what your problem is?

_____

_____

do and *did* for emphasis SB page 35

8 ★☆☆ **Match the sentences.**

1 Lucy did go to your party. ☐
2 I did enjoy that meal. ☐
3 Paul did seem a little strange. ☐
4 I do wish you'd turn down your music. ☐
5 Jen looks great in that dress. ☐
6 I do really like you. ☐

a Is there anything wrong with him?
b I'm trying to study.
c Green does suit her.
d She was wearing a red dress – remember?
e But not enough to be your girlfriend, sorry.
f But I think I ate too much.

9 ★★☆ **Rewrite the sentences adding *do/does* or *did* to make them more emphatic. Make any other necessary changes.**

0 So you like my present! I thought you didn't.
   So you do like my present! I thought you didn't.

1 You know Alan. You met him at Steve's party, remember?

_____

2 We spend a lot of our time talking about the same things. It's getting a bit boring.

_____

3 My dad embarrasses me sometimes but I guess all dads do.

_____

4 I don't know what May said but I enjoyed your party.

_____

5 Miss Holloway's great but she talks a lot.

_____

6 I've hardly got any money left. We bought a lot of things today.

_____

7 I miss my mum when she travels abroad for work.

_____

GET IT RIGHT!

so and *such*

Learners often confuse *so* and *such*.

✓ *We had no idea that we were going to become **such** good friends.*

✗ *We had no idea that we were going to become so good friends.*

✓ *Luke's parents aren't **so** strict.*

✗ *Luke's parents aren't such strict.*

Find four mistakes in the text. Correct them.

Bringing up children is not an easy job and some parents can be such strict that their children sometimes rebel. There is so a lot of advice out there about raising children that it's not always easy to make the right decisions. Amy Chua's book was such interesting I read it twice and it contained so many useful pieces of advice. Childhood is so a significant time in your life and it's so important to get things right.

VOCABULARY

Costumes and uniforms

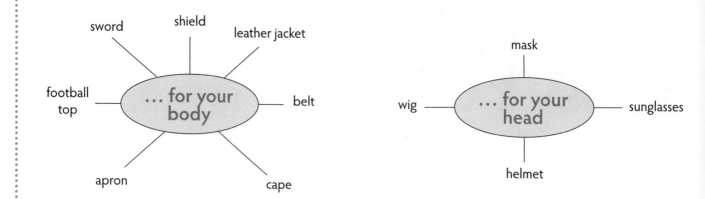

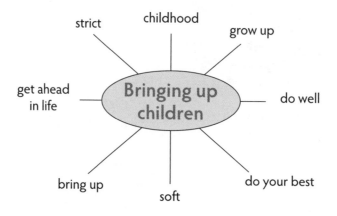

Key words in context

collection	My brother's got a huge **collection** of football shirts.
doorstep	Don't stand there on the **doorstep**. Come in.
fancy-dress	Have you decided what costume to wear to the **fancy-dress** party?
farewell	It's always sad to say **farewell** to colleagues who you've worked with for a number of years.
genius	They're a family of **geniuses**. They're all so intelligent.
ordinary	I'm just an **ordinary** kid like everyone else.
parenting	Good **parenting** is a real skill.
provocative	That was a **provocative** thing to say. Are you looking for an argument?

Costumes and uniforms `SB page 32`

1 ★☆☆ **Unscramble the words to make costumes and uniforms. Then match the words with the pictures.**

1 giw _____
2 tleb _____
3 sesnuslags _____

4 mehtle _____
5 words _____
6 smak _____

7 delish _____
8 pace _____
9 napor _____

 A ☐
 B ☐
 C ☐
 D ☐
 E ☐

 F ☐ G ☐

 H ☐
 I ☐

2 ★★☆ **Complete the story with words from Exercise 1.**

An invitation to a fancy dress party. Cool! What was I going to wear? I thought about going as a chef but Dad's ¹_____ was filthy and I didn't have time to wash it. What about a knight? I could use a stick as a ²_____ and a dustbin lid as a ³_____ but what about a ⁴_____ to wear on my head? No, a knight was too difficult. Then I thought about going as a superhero, a ⁵_____ to cover my face, a big ⁶_____ around my waist and a ⁷_____ over the top. Not bad but then I had a brilliant idea …

I arrived at Mike's house and knocked on the door. I was a rock star and I looked cool! Dark ⁸_____ hiding my eyes, a ⁹_____ of long black hair on my head and my dad's leather jacket.

Mike opened the door dressed in a suit and tie. Tina, his girlfriend was stood beside him in a beautiful dress. He looked at me and laughed. 'When I said dress fancy, I meant dress *smart*,' he laughed. It was too late now. I had to go in …

Bringing up children `SB page 35`

3 ★☆☆ **Match the phrases and the definitions.**

1 do well ☐
2 strict ☐
3 do your best ☐
4 bring up ☐
5 soft ☐
6 childhood ☐
7 grow up ☐
8 get ahead in life ☐

a to try your hardest
b to raise (children)
c to describe a parent who doesn't impose a lot of rules on their children
d to be successful
e to get older
f to describe a parent who imposes a lot of rules on their children
g to make good progress at school, in your job, etc.
h the period of your life until the age of 18

4 ★★☆ **Circle the correct option.**

1 All parents want to help their children *get ahead in life / grow up*.
2 It doesn't matter if you win or lose, as long as you *do well / do your best*.
3 I had a really happy *childhood / bring up*.
4 It was difficult for my dad *growing / bringing* up three children on his own.
5 She *did / made* really well in her final exam.
6 They can do whatever they want. Their parents are really *soft / strict*.
7 My little cousin is *growing / bringing* up really quickly.
8 My parents are so *soft / strict*. They don't let me do anything.

READING

1 REMEMBER AND CHECK **Correct the mistakes in these sentences. Then check your answers on page 31 of the Student's Book.**

1 Dale stood at the garden gate to wave Rain off.

_____

2 Dale wore fancy dress to wave Rain off to school on his first day at high school.

_____

3 Rain saw that his dad was dressed as an American football player as he was climbing onto the bus.

_____

_____

4 Dale waved Rain off only when the weather was good.

_____

5 Dale got a lot of his costumes from a fancy-dress shop.

_____

6 Rochelle Price took short videos of her husband to put on their website.

_____

_____

7 Rain never really appreciated what his dad did.

_____

8 Dale is looking forward to waving at the bus when school starts after the summer holidays.

_____

_____

2 **Read the magazine article. Who is it written by?**

A A parent with a difficult teen at home
B A young person with a difficult problem
C Someone who understands typical teenage issues

3 **Match the titles with the paragraphs. There are two extra titles.**

1 Try and be more understanding
2 Don't get too upset
3 Collect the evidence
4 They don't even know why they do it
5 Choose the behaviour you find most embarrassing
6 Have a family meeting

4 **Write a short text describing a problem you had with your parents and how you solved it.**

How to survive ... embarrassing parents

Don't get me wrong – I love my parents to bits. I know they love me too and would do anything to help me but sometimes they can be well ... really embarrassing. Dad wanting to pick me up from school, Mum getting over-excited when she watches me playing football for the school team. And I know it's not just me. My friends all moan about theirs from time to time. It seems a few cruel parents deliberately want to see their kids suffer, but others are just trying to be cool and fit in with our friends. Either way, they can make life pretty tricky for us at times. There's not really much we can do about it, or is there? Here are a few tips I've come up with to make life just a little easier for all of us.

A _____

Write a list of all the things you find embarrassing and then put them in order. Is the fact that your dad sings along to the radio when your friends are over for dinner worse than the fact that he always calls your best friend by the wrong name? By deciding which ones are worse means you'll be free to focus your energy where you need it most.

B _____

When you've decided which issues you want to talk about, keep a diary of all the times your mum or dad do the things that embarrass you most. When, where and how you felt – make a note of all these things. They'll help you put your case across.

C _____

When you've got enough evidence, it's time for a little face-to-face chat. Use your notes to help you. The chances are that even if your parents are conscious of doing these things, they probably don't realise how embarrassing they are. Keep calm. Let them know how you feel and why. Let them have their say – they'll probably want to defend themselves. Of course, you'll also have to be prepared to listen to some of the things that they're not so keen on about your behaviour. It's part of the deal. Maybe you can both agree to think more carefully about some of your actions.

D _____

Hopefully your parents will listen and be willing to change their ways, especially if you say you're happy to change too. Of course, sometimes they might not. When this happens then the best advice I can offer is to ignore it and get on with your life. If you do this, things will be a lot easier. Remember that they once had their own embarrassing parents, and the chances are many of us will be embarrassing parents ourselves one day. Maybe we shouldn't be too hard on them.

DEVELOPING WRITING

An essay about the role of grandparents

1 Read the essay and answer the questions.

1 Why does the writer think grandparents are more active in their grandchildren's lives these days?

2 Why can this be a good thing?

3 What should parents be careful about?

Grandparents can play an important part in children's lives. Do you agree?

Because of the high costs of professional child care, more and more parents in the UK are relying on their own mothers and fathers to look after their children so that they can go back to work. This means that these grandparents are getting to spend far more time with their grandchildren than their own parents did, but is this always a good thing?

Of course, grandparents can be a wonderful influence in a child's life. No one, except for their own parents, can love them more and the children will generally be well cared for. The time and attention that the child receives will help them grow up securely, knowing that they are special. This relationship often continues in later years and many teenagers have a close bond with their grandparents, knowing that they can turn to them with problems they won't always want to share with their parents.

But parents shouldn't abuse this situation. Parents should always be the most important influence in any child's life. They need to be there and make the important decisions rather than rely upon their own mothers and fathers to do so for them.

To sum up, children who grow up having a close relationship with their grandparents are very lucky indeed. However, their parents must be careful not to forget their responsibility for their child's upbringing and happiness.

2 Complete these sentences from the essay with the missing words. Then check in the text. What effect do these words have on the sentences?

1 This means that these grandparents are getting to spend _____ more time with their grandchildren than their own parents did.

2 _____ _____, grandparents can be a wonderful influence in a child's life.

3 Parents should _____ be the most important influence in any child's life.

4 To sum up, children who grow up having a close relationship with their grandparents are very lucky _____.

3 Use the missing words from Exercise 2 to make these sentences more emphatic. Sometimes there is more than one possibility.

1 You must think of the child's safety.

_____

2 It's more difficult to spend all day looking after young children.

_____

3 Grandparents love their grandchildren very much.

_____

4 Grandparents want to help their own children.

4 Make notes to answer the questions.

1 What is the role of grandparents in your society?

2 What is good about the situation?

3 Is there anything to be careful about?

4 What are your thoughts?

5 Use your notes to write an answer to the essay question in about 200 words.

CHECKLIST ✓

☐ Include an attention-grabbing introduction

☐ Organise your ideas in a logical sequence

☐ Include examples of emphatic language

☐ Read through your essay to check for mistakes

LISTENING

1 🔊08 Listen and write the name of the embarrassed daughter (Jen, Sue or Dawn) under the picture of the dad.

 A ☐

 B ☐

 C ☐

2 🔊08 Listen again and mark the sentences T (true) or F (false).

1 Jen never needs a lift from her dad. ☐

2 Jen's mum is sympathetic to her daughter's complaint. ☐

3 Sue thinks her dad's hairstyle is old-fashioned. ☐

4 Sue's mum is sympathetic to her daughter's complaint. ☐

5 Dawn's taste in music has changed. ☐

6 Dawn's mum is sympathetic to her daughter's complaint. ☐

3 🔊08 Make the sentences more emphatic by rewriting them with *do*, *so* or *such* in the correct form. Listen again and check.

1 Dad knows how to embarrass me.

_____

2 We're your parents, Jen, we care about you.

_____

3 It's an inappropriate hairstyle for a man of his age.

_____

4 Dad's embarrassing.

_____

5 I liked it when I was about eight.

_____

DIALOGUE

1 Put the dialogue in order.

☐ DAD Well it's our house and we like to keep it just a little bit tidy.

☐ DAD It's your bedroom. It's such a mess. Again.

☐ DAD Because maybe when I go to check your room in half an hour it will be perfect.

☐ DAD Very funny, Paul. Now I did say that if your room was a mess, I wouldn't give you your pocket money this month.

[1] DAD You do know how to annoy your mum, Paul.

☐ DAD I can but maybe I won't need to.

☐ PAUL It will be, Dad. Thanks for the second chance.

☐ PAUL Well, it's my bedroom so I don't see what the problem is.

☐ PAUL Why not?

☐ PAUL A bit tidy? This house is so tidy we could invite the Queen round for dinner.

☐ PAUL What have I done now?

☐ PAUL No way, Dad, you can't do that. I need the money.

2 Use the words in brackets to change the sentences and make them more emphatic.

MUM Why didn't you clean your room?

JAY But I cleaned it, Mum. (did)

1 _____

MUM Really? Last time I looked it was a mess. (such)

2 _____

JAY When was that?

MUM Five minutes ago!

JAY Well go and have a look now. It's tidy. You won't believe it. (so)

3 _____

MUM And if I look under the bed?

JAY Mum, you know how to be annoying, don't you? Just give me five more minutes then.

3 Write a short dialogue (6–10 lines) between a parent and child. Use at least two examples of emphatic language.

Pronunciation
Adding emphasis
Go to page 118. 🔊

Listening part 3

1 ◀》**10** You will hear five short extracts in which people are talking about family holidays. For questions 1–5, choose from the list (A–H) what each speaker says about them. Use the letters only once. There are three extra letters which you do not need to use.

A They're never as good as I hope they will be.

B They're usually very stressful.

C Everyone does what they want to do.

D My parents worry too much about showing us a good time.

E It's a good time to reconnect with everyone.

F Mum and Dad can never really relax on them.

G We never go to places that I want to go to.

H I think I've outgrown them.

Speaker 1 ☐
Speaker 2 ☐
Speaker 3 ☐
Speaker 4 ☐
Speaker 5 ☐

Exam guide: multiple matching

In this part of the exam you need to match speakers to a sentence describing part of what they are talking about.

- You hear five people talking about the same subject – they are not connected to each other. You hear each extract twice.

- On the exam paper there are eight comments. Your job is to match one to each of the speakers. There are three comments you won't use.

- Before you listen, read through the comments to prepare yourself for the sorts of things you will hear.

- You will need to listen out for attitudes, opinions, purpose, feelings, main points and details.

- Listen to each speaker carefully. You will sometimes hear things that are intended to distract you from the correct answer, so avoid making quick decisions.

- Use your second listening to confirm answers you have already chosen and answer those questions you weren't able to the first time round.

2 ◀》**11** You will hear five short extracts in which people are answering the question, 'What is the most important role of a parent?' For questions 1–5, choose from the list (A–H) what each speaker says about it. Use the letters only once. There are three extra letters which you do not need to use.

A Parents need to ensure that they supply their children with the fundamental requirements.

B Parents have to expect they will have difficult times with their teenage children.

C Parents need to teach their children values.

D Survival skills are the most important thing a parent can pass on to their child.

E Parents can never be really good friends with their children.

F The most important part of being a parent comes naturally.

G It's very difficult to choose which role is most essential.

H Parents need to take more responsibility.

Speaker 1 ☐
Speaker 2 ☐
Speaker 3 ☐
Speaker 4 ☐
Speaker 5 ☐

4 THINKING OUTSIDE THE BOX

GRAMMAR

be / get used to (doing) vs. used to (do) SB page 40

1 ★☆☆ **Complete with the correct form of the verb given (infinitive or -ing form).**

1 That fast food place used to _____ my favourite French restaurant. (be)

2 When I first lived in a flat I couldn't get used to _____ our neighbour's music. (hear)

3 My mother has finally got used to _____ the Internet on her phone. (have)

4 Pedro comes from Brazil, so he isn't used to _____ British food. (eat)

5 Sheila used to _____ jeans all the time when she was a student. (wear)

6 We live near the palace and we're very used to _____ members of the royal family going past. (see)

7 I wonder if I'll ever get used to _____ in such a beautiful place. (live)

8 When we arrived in London, we weren't used to _____ in so much traffic. (drive)

2 ★★☆ **Circle the correct option.**

When I was young I ¹used to / got used to play outside with my friends. My mum ²used to / was used to me going out to ride my bike with them. Sometimes I was out for hours, but she ³used to / got used to that, too. We often rode on mud tracks that ⁴used to / were used to be used by motorcyclists, and they were often wet and slippery so I ⁵used to / got used to falling off my bike a lot. And so my mum ⁶used to / was used to seeing me covered with mud and bruises.

Now I ⁷used to / am used to driving safely in my car and staying clean! I don't think I could ⁸be used to / get used to riding a bike again now.

3 ★★☆ **Complete the sentences with the correct form of be or get.**

1 Julia is Mexican so she _____ used to hot weather.

2 My uncle's working in Berlin, so he had to _____ used to different food.

3 It never takes me long to _____ used to being in another country.

4 My father lived in Italy for years, but he never _____ used to driving on the right.

5 My grandmother _____ used to living in her small flat now, and she's very happy.

6 Bernard grew up in Norway. As a child he _____ used to skiing to school.

7 I like warm weather. I could never _____ used to very cold winters.

8 People in some parts of Japan _____ used to experiencing earthquakes – they happen quite often.

9 On holiday, I went to the beach every day. That's something I could easily _____ used to!

4 ★★★ **Complete the statements. Make them true for you.**

1 When I was younger I used to _____

2 When I started school it wasn't easy to get used to _____

3 Now I am used to _____

4 My best friend was used to _____
   before I met him/her.

5 My parents have never got used to _____

Adverbs and adverbial phrases
SB page 43

5 ★☆☆ **Complete the sentences with the adverb formed from the adjective in brackets.**

0 The horse jumped over all the barriers *easily* . (easy)

1 The car was going too _____ for the police to catch up with. (fast)

2 The singer sang the song _____ . (beautiful)

3 Matty didn't do the test _____ enough to get top marks. (good)

4 My eyes _____ became accustomed to the dim light. (slow)

5 Sam worked really _____ to finish the job on time. (hard)

6 ★☆☆ **Complete the sentences with a word from the list.**

enjoyable | different | surprise | friendly
interest | excitement | fear | strange

1 We really like Ms Philips, she teaches PE in an _____ way.

2 We all jumped with _____ when the door slammed.

3 She came second, but she congratulated the winner in a _____ way.

4 The fans screamed with _____ when the pop group walked onto the stage.

5 Nobody understood the teacher's explanation of calculus, until he explained it in a _____ way.

6 Fran started to shake with _____ when she looked over the edge of the cliff.

7 The dog was walking in a _____ way because he had hurt his paw.

8 Harry told us a long, boring story which we listened to without much _____ .

7 ★★★ **Complete the sentences with a phrase. Make them true for you.**

1 I watch _____ on TV _____

2 I do my homework _____

3 I read books _____

4 I always try to _____ in a friendly way.

5 I like to _____ in a different way.

6 I admire people who _____ without fear.

7 I know someone who walks _____

8 I go to the maths class _____

8 ★★★ **Write complete sentences from the prompts. Use adverbial phrases and make any other necessary changes.**

0 Mary / ask / her hairdresser / style / her hair / different

   Mary asked her hairdresser to style her hair in a different way.

1 Jack / approach / lion / fear

2 Candy / carry / three suitcases / difficulty

3 The boys / eat / hamburgers / enthusiasm

4 Jerry / ride / horse / awkward

5 Helen / watch / football match / interest

GET IT RIGHT!
Adverbs

Learners often make word order errors with adverbs.

✓ *You can **easily find** a hotel.*

✗ *You can ~~find easily~~ a hotel.*

Put the words in order to make sentences.

1 finish / by / I'll / project / next / definitely / the / Monday

2 immediately / you / It's / thing / good / that / came / a

3 your / I / view / understand / point / totally / of

4 and / Dan / on / hard / his / got / worked / top / homework / marks

5 Jo and Kate / would / hear / quietly / so / speaking / no one / were / them

6 job / creatively / to / in / Do / always / think / have / your / you / ?

7 locally / so / I / home / walk / live / I / can

8 eaten / probably / pizza / the / This / I've / is / best / ever

VOCABULARY

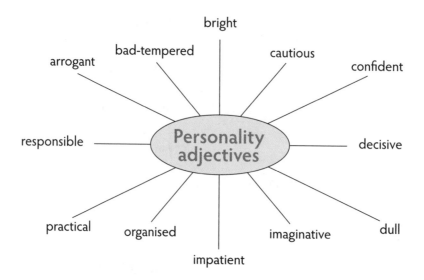

Common adverbial phrases

by accident
in a hurry
in a panic
in a row
in private
in public
in secret
on purpose

good

for good
it's a good thing
it's all good
it's no good
not very good at
so far, so good

Key words in context

anxious	I've never acted on stage before, so right now I'm a bit **anxious**.
brainstorm	We need some new, fresh ideas – let's **brainstorm** for ten minutes or so.
capable	Sometimes we find that we are **capable** of more things than we think we are.
charge	My phone battery's dead – I need to **charge** it.
conflict	They argue with each other all the time – there's a lot of **conflict** between them.
enthusiasm	She didn't really want to go, so she didn't watch the play with any **enthusiasm**.
flash	A police car went past with a blue **flashing** light on its roof.
on the basis (that)	We chose him for the basketball team **on the basis that** he was the tallest guy we knew.
scholarship	She isn't paying for her course because she won a **scholarship**.

Personality adjectives `SB page 40`

1 ★★☆ **Complete the puzzle. Read what each person says and write the adjective to describe the person. Find the mystery word.**

1 I learn quickly and easily.
2 I get lots of new ideas.
3 If I say I'll do something, then I do it.
4 I'm the best, by far!
5 I always think carefully before I do anything.
6 I'm sure of my abilities.
7 I don't sit around thinking for a long time.
8 I know where everything is.
9 I'm better at doing things than thinking about things.

Mystery word: 'I want it – and I want it now!'

---

2 ★★☆ **Complete with an appropriate adjective.**

1 A She gets angry at everything I say.
  B Oh, I know, she's quite _____.

2 A He drives quite slowly.
  B Yes, he's a _____ driver, usually.

3 A She designs such different, interesting things!
  B Yes, she's very _____.

4 A Let's go to Australia for our holiday.
  B Oh, be _____. We haven't got enough money for that.

5 A Do you think she'll do what she promised?
  B Oh yes – she's very _____.

6 A She thinks she's the best. I guess she's confident.
  B No, it's more than that – she's really _____.

7 A Hurry up!
  B OK. Don't be so _____!

8 A He isn't very interesting, is he?
  B No, he's a bit _____, really.

Common adverbial phrases `SB page 43`

3 ★☆☆ **Complete the sentences with the phrases in the list.**

by accident | in a hurry | in a panic | in a row
in public | in secret | on purpose | in private

1 Sorry, I can't stop and talk now – I'm
_____.

2 I made a mistake – I clicked the wrong button and deleted the file _____.

3 I'm a nervous person – I don't think I could ever make a speech _____.

4 Has any country ever won the World Cup three times _____?

5 I only ever sing _____ – in the shower, for example.

6 No one knew that the meetings were happening – they were held _____.

7 I was so worried about being late that I started to do everything _____.

8 I'm sorry I broke it, but I promise you, I didn't do it _____!

WordWise `SB page 45`

good

4 ★★☆ **Use phrases with good to complete the sentences.**

0 No school today, the sun's shining, I'm with my friends – *it's all good*.

1 She's not going to Australia just for a holiday – she's going there _____.

2 Oh, no! This food is awful! Well, I guess I'm _____ at cooking.

3 A It's really cold today.
  B Yes. _____ we're wearing our coats.

4 A How are you getting on?
  B _____. I think I'll finish in ten minutes.

5 I've apologised three times to her, but _____ – she's still angry with me.

5 ★★★ **Complete the sentences so that they are true for you.**

1 I'm not very good at _____.
2 It's a good thing that I _____.
3 I'm going to _____ for good.
4 I would really like to _____ but it's no good.

READING

1 REMEMBER AND CHECK **Mark the sentences T (true) or F (false). Then check your answers in the article on page 39 of the Student's Book.**

1 Richard is a member of the Zulu tribe. ☐
2 The tribe had problems because lions were killing people. ☐
3 Richard's first idea was to use fire to keep the lions away. ☐
4 The lions did not like a moving light. ☐

5 To make his light, Richard used a battery from an old motorbike. ☐
6 Richard designed a light that flashed all night. ☐
7 Lions no longer kill Richard's father's animals. ☐
8 Because of his idea, Richard now teaches at a college in the USA. ☐

2 Read the article. Find three things that Einstein believed in as being important for thinking.

Einstein's thinking

'The true sign of intelligence is not knowledge, but imagination.' *Albert Einstein*

For a lot of people, one of the best examples of creative genius was Albert Einstein, the physicist who came up with the Theory of Relativity, and by doing so, changed physics forever. However, what a lot of people don't know is that Einstein had specific techniques that he used to develop his ability to think creatively and freely.

Possibility thinking

The main approach that Einstein took was something he called 'possibility thinking' – in other words, letting yourself imagine things that are often way outside reality, and pushing the limits of what you know. It means getting away from our familiar thoughts and ideas and trying to imagine many other possible things, no matter how incredible they might seem.

Einstein had a special technique to do this, which he called 'the thought experiment'. This example of possibility thinking is simply an experiment that you do inside your own head. Perhaps the most famous thought experiment is the one that Einstein says he used to get himself on the path towards the Theory of Relativity. Einstein was interested in light and the speed of light and its relationship to time, so what he did was to imagine himself riding on a beam of sunlight. Now, that's an impossible thing to do, of course, but Einstein said that using his imagination like this allowed him to understand some of the relationships between light and time, and how they work.

Essentially, how we experience time depends on where we are and what we are doing. Einstein explained it as follows: 'When you're talking to a pretty girl, an hour seems like a minute. If you sit on a hot fire, a minute seems like an hour. That's relativity.'

Time for creative thinking

But importantly, for possibility thinking to be effective, we have to give ourselves opportunities to practise it. Lots of people say that their 'thinking time' is when they're taking a bath, or when they're on the bus to work or school. But Einstein believed that it is important to devote a period of time every day to 'creative thinking': whatever problem or idea it is that interests you, set aside some time every day to thinking about it – concentrated thinking. And he was a great believer in images, too – he said that he often thought 'in a stream of pictures', and that this was a powerful way to think.

Einstein also believed in thinking about a problem for a long time and not giving up: as he once said, 'I think and think for months and years. Ninety-nine times, the conclusion is false. The hundredth time I am right.'

3 Read the article again. Match the sentence halves.

1 Einstein is known as the genius who ☐
2 Not everybody knows that Einstein ☐
3 Possibility thinking means ☐
4 Einstein came up with an image ☐
5 The image helped him ☐
6 Possibility thinking only really works ☐
7 Einstein felt that thinking in pictures ☐
8 Einstein thought it was important ☐

a develop his Theory of Relativity.
b to keep thinking until you get the answer.
c first thought of the Theory of Relativity.
d had things that he did to help him think freely.
e was something very powerful.
f of himself travelling on a beam of light.
g moving away from the ways that we usually think.
h if we practise it regularly.

4 When and where are you able to think the most freely? Write a short paragraph.

Pronunciation
Pronouncing words with *gh*
Go to page 119.

DEVELOPING WRITING

Writing an email of advice

1 **Read Marnie's email. What does she want her sister Becca to do?**

Hi Becca,

[A] How are things with you? How's it going at university? I hope you're enjoying everything and not working too hard!

[B] Well, you know that I'm going to be doing my end-of-year exams soon, right? Just like you did all those years ago. Well, I'm writing to ask you for some advice. The thing is, I just can't get going with revision, because I'm really busy with lots of things at school and at home. Now, I know that revision's really, really important, but I'm finding that days are going past and I'm not fitting it in. It's really frustrating. I try to organise my time, but it's hopeless! I'm just useless at it. I also don't really have any techniques for it and I think I'll never come up with anything.

[C] Have you got any tips you can give me?

[D] Now, I know you're busy too but I'm hoping you can find a few minutes to help your sweet younger sister out! The thing is, I don't know who else to ask.

See you soon I hope!

Love

Marnie

---

2 **Match the underlined phrases in the email to the definitions.**

1 We use this phrase to introduce our main concern or problem. _____

2 We use this phrase to start talking about something the reader/listener already knows. _____

3 We use this word to give emphasis to what we are about to say. _____

4 We use this word to signal we're going to talk about something important. _____

3 **Use the underlined phrases in the email to complete the sentences.**

1 Sandra – _____ there's a test tomorrow, right?

2 I'd like to give you some advice, but _____, I'm no good at revision myself!

3 So why am I writing? _____, because you asked for my advice, of course!

4 _____, you might not like all these ideas, but I'm going to send them anyway.

4 **Match the information to the paragraphs A–D.**

1 The main body of the email – the problem. ☐

2 Explaining that you don't want to cause the person a lot of problems, and why you're writing. ☐

3 Saying what you want the reader to do. ☐

4 Some personal exchange about the other person's life. ☐

5 **Here are some ideas of how to help Marnie. Add two more ideas of your own. Cross through any that you don't like.**

- Revise early in the day; it's better than at night.
- Make a timetable for every day. Tell other people when you're going to do revision.
- Ask someone to test you as soon as you've done some revision.
- Make sure to be away from computers, laptops, tablets, etc. when you revise.
- Put revision notes around the house so you keep seeing them.
- Keep as healthy as you can.
- _____
- _____

6 **Imagine you are Becca. Write your reply to Marnie. Use your ideas in Exercise 5. Write 150–200 words.**

CHECKLIST ✔

☐ Use a structure for an email

☐ Include some personal exchanges in your introduction

☐ Use some expressions from Exercise 3

☐ Give the most useful advice and say why

☐ Close the email in a friendly way, e.g. *Good luck! / I'm sure you'll do great / I hope this is helpful*

LISTENING

1 🔊 14 **Listen and write the number of the conversation next to the correct picture.**

2 🔊 14 **Listen again and complete the summaries of the conversations. Use between 1 and 3 words.**

Conversation 1

The man is trying to ¹_____ his anorak but he can't. The woman offers to help, but he decides to try again. Then he begins to ²_____ so the woman tells him to calm down. Then she tries but she can't ³_____ either. So he decides to ⁴_____ his head but it gets ⁵_____ again. The woman laughs.

Conversation 2

A boy who is painting asks his friend for her opinion. She says it isn't ⁶_____ his last one. Then she admits that ⁷_____ that good. The boy says that he's going to ⁸_____ painting but the girl tries to persuade him not to. But he says that he will ⁹_____ photography and never wants to ¹⁰_____ paints and brushes again.

Conversation 3

A woman needs to think of ¹¹_____ for her company. She has to have them for a meeting ¹²_____ morning, but she's stuck. And she's worried because ¹³_____ o'clock and she might have to ¹⁴_____ late. Her friend starts to tell her about ¹⁵_____ thinking, but she isn't interested so he ¹⁶_____ to it.

DIALOGUE

1 **Put the dialogues in the correct order.**

1

	JEAN	I'm doing a crossword puzzle and I've only got three answers left to find.
1	JEAN	This is so frustrating!
	JEAN	No chance! I can't give up like that. That would be cheating.
	JEAN	Oh, that's OK. I always prefer to do them on my own, anyway. But I'm really stuck right now.
	MARCUS	A crossword? I'm no good at those. I can't help you, I'm afraid.
	MARCUS	OK then. Well, good luck, tell me when you've finished it!
	MARCUS	What is it? What are you trying to do?
	MARCUS	Well, if you're stuck, why don't you just look at the answers? No one will know!

2

	ELLA	Yes, I am. Well, I'm trying to. But to be honest, I can't do it.
	ELLA	Oh, don't be like that. You're good at these things, usually.
1	ELLA	Hello? James, is that you?
	ELLA	Well, now I give up. I was hoping you might help me! That's why I called.
	JAMES	I know I am. That's why I'm so frustrated. I've tried everything, but it's hopeless.
	JAMES	Hi, Ella. How are you? Are you doing the homework?
	JAMES	I'm stuck, too. I'll never get it right, I'm sure.
	JAMES	Sorry, but there you go. I'll see you tomorrow, Ella. Bye.

PHRASES FOR FLUENCY `SB page 45`

1 **Circle the correct options.**

1 A This is terrible. I'm starting to panic!
  B OK, *just calm down / you can't be serious*, it'll be OK.

2 A Your hair looks awful!
  B You know, *you're really out of order / that's just it* when you say things like that.

3 A It's so difficult to find a good babysitter these days.
  B *That's just it / Give it a rest*, no one's available at short notice!

4 A Come on, write it down.
  B Sorry, but how do you spell it *off / again*?

5 A Honestly – my dad was an international footballer!
  B Oh, *calm down / give it a rest*!

6 A I'm going for a swim in the sea.
  B But it's freezing! *You're out of order / You can't be serious*!

Writing part 2

1 Read the exam task. Then read Roberta's letter. Circle the most appropriate options (not too informal).

> Next month you're going to stay with an English-speaking family on an exchange programme. The family's mother has written to you and asked you to say if there's anything she needs to know about you before you go and stay. Write your response.

> [1] *Hi / Dear* Mrs Stevens,
>
> [2] *Thank you so much / Thanks a lot* for your really kind letter. It was nice to hear from you and I'm really looking forward to meeting you next month.
>
> [3] *Just thought I'd drop you a line / I'm writing now* because you asked me if there was anything you should know before I come. Well, I'm quite an easy-going person, so I don't think I'm going to be much trouble! But there are [4] *a couple of / two* things that I'd like you to know.
>
> First of all, I sometimes have trouble sleeping and that's especially true if the bedroom isn't very dark. When we go away, I sometimes take an eye-mask with me, but I don't find it comfortable. So, if my room could be nice and dark, that would be [5] *great / cool*.
>
> The other thing is food — [6] *I'm not very keen on / I really can't stand* spicy food. So if you are all curry fans, I'm afraid I might have to pass! But otherwise, I'll eat [7] *any old stuff / almost anything*. (Oh, except mushrooms — sorry!)
>
> I hope this is helpful — please let me know if you need anything else before I arrive.
>
> [8] *Best wishes / See you soon*
>
> Roberta

2 Read these phrases that people use in letters/emails. Circle the one in each pair that is more formal.

1. A Great to hear from you!
   B Thank you for your letter.
2. A I hope you're well.
   B How are things with you?
3. A Is there anything else I can tell you?
   B What else do you want to know?
4. A I think that's everything.
   B OK, I'm going to wrap up now.
5. A See you!
   B I hope to see you soon.

3 Use the letter to find the answers to the questions Roberta asked herself before writing.

1. How can I reassure Mrs Stevens that there aren't any problems?

   _____

2. Should I tell her about my sleeping problem?

   _____

3. What, if anything, do I want to say about food? Do I mention spicy food and mushrooms?

   _____

4. How can I end the letter in a nice way?

   _____

Exam guide: writing a neutral/less informal letter

In part 2 you have to answer one of three questions. You have to write an article, an email/letter, an essay, a review or a story in 140–190 words.

- Think about who you are writing to and the kind of language you should use.
- Plan what you want to say and how you will organise the content of your letter.
- Make sure you start and end the letter with appropriate expressions.
- Make sure you include anything the task tells you to include.

4 Read the letter-writing task below. Plan and write your letter in 140–190 words.

> You spent some time studying English in a school in Britain or the USA. You have received this letter from the school director. Write your answer in 140–190 words in an appropriate style.

> Dear ...
>
> I am writing to tell you that your exam results have arrived – you got an A. Congratulations, it's a great result!
>
> I was wondering if you would like to return to us here at the school, and study for the examination at the next level up. We feel sure you would do very well in it.
>
> Please write and let me know.
>
> Best wishes
>
> Julia Stevenson

Write your letter.

CONSOLIDATION

LISTENING

1 🔊 **15** **Listen to Paul talking about his childhood and circle the correct answers.**

1 Who used to argue the most in his family home?
   A Paul with his parents
   B Paul with his sister and brother
   C Paul's mum with his dad

2 What did Paul think was great about how his parents raised him?
   A They weren't very strict with him.
   B They always had clear expectations.
   C They were always happy to play board games.

3 How did they treat his friends?
   A They weren't very friendly.
   B They were too interfering with them.
   C They wanted to know about them as people.

2 🔊 **15** **Listen again and mark the sentences T (true) or F (false).**

1 Paul doesn't remember his parents ever fighting. ☐

2 Paul thinks his parents were too strict at times. ☐

3 Paul couldn't join in with some of the conversations in the school playground. ☐

4 Paul's parents encouraged him to be active. ☐

5 Paul's dad would sometimes embarrass him. ☐

GRAMMAR

3 **Put the words in order to make sentences.**

1 own / The / of / tablet / friends / vast / my / majority / have / their

   _____

2 board game / We / enough / tonight / players / got / for / haven't / the

   _____

3 that / so / fix / practical / he / anything / He / can / is

   _____

4 to / I / do / do / listening / nothing / to / when / I've / music / enjoy / got

   _____

5 never / I'll / early / to / waking / used / up / get / so

   _____

6 teaches / White / way / chemistry / an / Mr / enjoyable / in

   _____

VOCABULARY

4 **Choose the correct options.**

1 We didn't recognise him because he was wearing a *mask* / *belt*.

2 Steve is so *arrogant* / *cautious*. He thinks he's better than all of us.

3 Knights carried a *shield* / *sword* to protect themselves from arrows.

4 Cyclists should wear *an apron* / *a helmet* to protect their head.

5 My dad's not very *confident* / *decisive*. He can never make up his mind.

6 He hasn't got any hair so he wears a *cape* / *wig*.

7 Don't be so *impatient* / *dull*. I'll be ready to go in five minutes.

8 Her teachers says she's very *responsible* / *bright* and should go on to university.

5 **Match the sentences.**

1 My dad's not very strict. ☐
2 Your homework's full of silly mistakes. ☐
3 I had a really happy childhood. ☐
4 He didn't do that by accident. ☐
5 Bring your children up as well as you can. ☐
6 She's a very secretive woman. ☐
7 Our football team's doing really well. ☐
8 Always try and do your best at school. ☐

a It will help you get ahead in life.
b It will help them do well in life.
c He did it on purpose.
d She lives her life in private.
e In fact he's quite soft actually.
f They've won five games in a row now.
g I grew up with a lot of love and care.
h You did it in a hurry, didn't you?

DIALOGUE

6 Put the dialogue in the correct order.

☐	DAD	OK, calm down. You always give up too easily.
☐	DAD	What do you mean, give up? What do you have to do?
☐	DAD	Music and art. That sounds perfect for you.
1	DAD	What's the matter, Oscar?
☐	DAD	That's a bit out of order. I'm only trying to help.
☐	DAD	No you're not. You just need a good idea.

☐	OSCAR	I have to design a CD cover for my favourite band.
☐	OSCAR	I know. I'm sorry, Dad. Maybe I just need a bit of a break.
☐	OSCAR	That's the problem, Dad. I just can't come up with anything. It's hopeless!
☐	OSCAR	Leave it out, Dad. Just leave me alone.
6	OSCAR	That's what I thought. But I'm useless.
☐	OSCAR	It's this school art project. I give up.

READING

7 Read the article and answer the questions.

A work-life balance

For a lot of parents, getting the balance between family life and work is a difficult thing to do. Of course, all parents want to spend time with their children and watch them grow up but at the same time there is the need to make money to provide for the family. Being at work usually means being away from the family and this is often a source of guilt for working mums and dads. One such parent was Mohamed El-Erian.

One night when he asked his ten-year-old daughter to go and brush her teeth before bed, he could have hardly known that it would eventually lead to him resigning as the boss of one of the biggest financial companies in the world.

It seemed that his daughter was ignoring his request and although he asked her several times she just stayed doing what she was doing. Clearly this annoyed her father who wanted to know why she was behaving so badly. When he pointed out that there was a time when she would have obeyed him immediately with no question, she asked him to wait a minute while she fetched something from her bedroom.

What she brought back would make him re-evaluate his life forever, because it was a list of 22 of the most important occasions in her life that he had been absent from. Among them were her first day at school, parents' evening at her school, her first match in the school football team and a holiday parade.

Mohamed immediately had to reassess his life. His high-profile job involved an incredible amount of time out of the house as he arrived in his office each day at 4.15 am and returned home only at 7 pm in time to kiss his daughter good night.

As he read through the list he also realised that he had had an excuse for missing each of the events; an important phone call, travel, urgent meetings, sudden problems that needed his direct involvement. He knew that he had lost control of the balance between his work and his family and that he was neglecting to give his daughter the time and attention that he knew she needed.

As a result he resigned from his job in order to spend more quality time with his family. Although he still works within the industry, he makes sure that he has the flexibility to always be around when he is needed.

Mohamed was just lucky that he got his warning before it was too late and he'd missed his daughter's childhood completely.

1 What was it about his daughter's behaviour that concerned Mohamed El-Erian?

2 How did his daughter respond to his complaint?

3 What excuses did he give for missing the key moments in her life?

4 What did his daughter's list help him realise?

5 How has his life changed?

WRITING

8 Write a paragraph of about 120 words about an occasion in a child's life that no parent should ever miss. Say:

- what the occasion is
- why it's so important
- why the parents should be there

5 | SCREEN TIME

GRAMMAR

Obligation, permission and prohibition (review) `SB page 50`

1 ★☆☆ **Circle the correct verbs to complete the sentences.**

1 You *don't have to / aren't supposed to* eat too many sweet things. They're bad for your teeth.
2 He *didn't let me / didn't need to* buy a new tablet. He already had one.
3 We *are not allowed to / had better* eat in the library. It's not permitted.
4 My parents *don't let me / allow me to* use my computer after 8 pm. They don't want me to spend all evening on it.
5 We *have to / don't have to* turn off our phones in school. We can't use them in class.
6 You *had better / shouldn't* spend all evening texting your friends. Do something else instead.

2 ★★☆ **Complete the sentences with the modal verbs in the list.**

aren't allowed to | had better | mustn't
didn't have to | made | didn't let

1 'You have to wear a hat and scarf today. It's cold.'
My mum _____ me wear a hat and scarf today.
2 'You have to get to school early tomorrow. The coach leaves at 8 am.'
I _____ be late to school tomorrow morning.
3 'You can't bring your dog into this restaurant.'
We _____ take our dog into the restaurant.
4 'I really need a new school jumper. This one is too small.'
I _____ buy a new jumper.
5 'You can't go to the cinema tonight.'
My dad _____ us go to the cinema last night.
6 'It wasn't necessary for Tom to lend me his tablet.'
Tom _____ lend me his tablet.

3 ★★★ **Unscramble the sentences to complete the dialogues. Use the correct form of the verbs.**

1 A Why haven't you got your mobile phone with you today?
  B mum / My / make / it / leave / me / at / home
  _____

2 A Why didn't you come climbing on Saturday?
  B parents / My / not allow / to / me / go
  _____

3 A Are you ready to go yet?
  B No, I can't find my Geography homework.
  A had better / You / find / it / soon
  _____
  The class has already started.

4 A Why were you late yesterday?
  B have to / I / my / Sorry, / bedroom / tidy
  _____

5 A I gave Joanna my phone yesterday.
  B must not / you / But / give / phone / your / anyone / to
  _____

6 A Did you see the match last night?
  B stay / it / parents / No, / up / not let / my / me / for
  _____

4 ★★★ **Complete the sentences so that they are true for you. Choose from the verbs in the list and give a reason.**

must / mustn't | let / don't let
have to / don't have to | should / shouldn't
allowed to / not allowed to

1 My parents _____ me play on the tablet as much as I want because _____
2 I _____ use my mobile phone too much because _____
3 I _____ have a TV in my bedroom because _____
4 I _____ think carefully before I post photos of friends and family because _____

Necessity: *(didn't) need to / needn't have* SB page 51

5 ★☆☆ **Match the statements and responses.**

1 The battery for my laptop has run out. ☐
2 I don't have enough space on my hard drive. ☐
3 I didn't have a European plug. ☐
4 We were late yesterday. ☐
5 I arrived an hour before the concert. ☐
6 I bought a Spanish dictionary yesterday. ☐
7 I failed my History exam. ☐
8 My friends keep texting me. I can't work. ☐

a You needn't have left home so early.
b You needed to take an earlier bus.
c I've got one. You needn't have bought one.
d You need to get a charger.
e Turn your phone off. You need to finish your homework.
f You needed to do more revision for it.
g You needed to get an adaptor.
h You need to delete some files.

6 ★★☆ **Read the situations. Then make comments with *didn't need to* or *needn't have*.**

0 I bought two concert tickets. My friend had already bought them.
   I needn't have bought the tickets.

1 Daniel didn't do his homework last night. He'd already done it the night before.

2 Sally didn't revise for her History exam. She passed it easily anyway.

3 I took a thick jumper with me yesterday but it was a hot, sunny day.

4 Lucy cooked Brian a birthday cake but his mum had already bought him one from the shops.

5 Liam didn't have dinner at home because he knew there was food at the party.

6 We took a taxi from the station but the hotel was only 200 metres away so we could have walked there.

7 I'd already sent Lara a text and that's why I didn't call her.

Ability in the past: *could, was / were able to, managed to, succeeded in doing* SB page 53

7 ★★☆ **Write sentences using the prompts.**

0 I / not manage / mend / my phone / yet
   I haven't managed to mend my phone yet.

1 James / not succeed / pass / his driving test / yet

2 I / not able to / find / my charger / yet

3 Sarah / not able to / swim / yesterday

4 We / succeed / climb / Ben Nevis / at the weekend

5 They / not able to / access / the Internet / at / the hotel / last night

6 He / not have / much / time / but / he / manage to / finish / the project

GET IT RIGHT!

must

Learners often use *should, would,* and *can* instead of *must*.

✓ I **mustn't** forget to give you my phone number.

✗ I ~~shouldn't~~ forget to give you my phone number.

Choose the correct verb to complete the sentences.

1 We *can / must / would* admit that peer pressure can be a problem.

2 They *shouldn't / can't / mustn't* be using artificial flowers – it doesn't look nice.

3 I really *can / would / must* get a new headset; this one doesn't work very well.

4 Harry *mustn't / can't / wouldn't* have arrived yet as his car isn't here.

5 To get this job applicants *can / should / must* be proficient speakers in Chinese. Non-Chinese speakers won't be considered.

6 *Should / Would / Must* you do that? It's highly irritating!

7 The children *wouldn't / mustn't / can't* arrive home late unless there was a problem.

8 The spectators *should / must / can* have seen the man run on stage. He ran right across it!

VOCABULARY

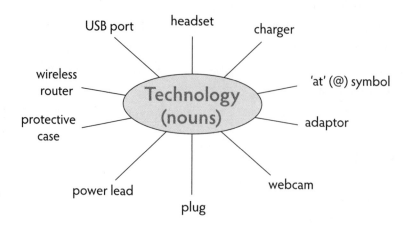

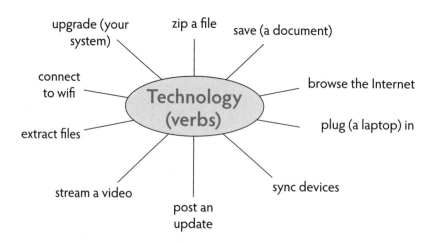

Key words in context

artificial	They're not real flowers. They're **artificial**. Look! They're plastic.
decade	In the last **decade**, technology has changed dramatically. I wonder what new technologies we'll see in the next ten years.
emigrate	Every year, thousands of people **emigrate** to another country.
excessive	Five hours a day online is an **excessive** amount of time. I'm not allowed to spend more than two hours.
influence	Max's performance of Dracula in the school play was **influenced** by Christopher Lee. Max has watched all the Christopher Lee films and he is a big fan.
launch	Facebook's website was **launched** on 4th February 2004.
motivate	My dad is a keen footballer and that **motivated** me to join my local football club.
peer pressure	There is **peer pressure** at school to have the latest smartphone.
proficient	My granddad is a **proficient** Internet user. He can do everything on the Internet now.

Technology (nouns) SB page 50

1 ★☆☆ **Unscramble the words and match them to the pictures.**

A ☐   B ☐   C ☐

D ☐   E ☐   F ☐

1 vetecitpro seac _____
2 ewmabc _____
3 gcerahr _____
4 woper dela _____
5 glup _____
6 dehates _____

2 ★★☆ **What do they need? Match the sentences (1–4) to (a–d).**

1 *I'm connecting my camera to my laptop.* ☐

2 *You need to include it in your email address.* ☐

3 *What do I need to connect to the wifi?* ☐

4 *You can't use a European plug here.* ☐

a wireless router   c USB port
b adaptor   d 'at' symbol

3 ★★☆ **Read the definitions. What are they?**

1 It provides access to the Internet or to a private computer network. _____

2 It stops my phone from being scratched or damaged. _____

3 It connects my laptop to the mains electricity.

_____

4 It holds an earphone and a microphone in place on your head. _____

5 You can use it to video chat over the Internet.

_____

Technology (verbs) SB page 51

4 ★★☆ **Read the clues and complete the puzzle with the missing verbs.**

1 We … interviews with our favourite singers.
2 My sister … updates on her blog once a week.
3 When I want to email big files, I always … them.
4 I'd better … my laptop in before the battery dies.
5 My dad usually … his phone every two years.
6 I need to learn how to … a file from a zipped folder.
7 I … all of my digital photos on my memory stick.
8 I want to … music from my laptop onto my phone.
9 You can find lots of interesting information when you … the Internet
10 If you go to the café on the High Street, you can … to the wifi for free.

5 ★★☆ **Complete the dialogues with the correct form of the technology verbs.**

zip | save | browse | connect | post | upgrade

1 A Have you _____ anything interesting on your blog this week?
  B No, I haven't had time.
2 A You've had the same phone for years. You should _____ it for a newer model.
  B I don't want to. I'm happy with this one.
3 A You look tired.
  B I am. I _____ the Internet for hours last night.
4 A I've got no space left on my hard drive.
  B You should _____ some of the large files. That will free up some space.
5 A How do I _____ my games console to the Internet?
  B You need access to a wireless connection.
6 A There isn't enough space to _____ all my music and photos on my hard drive.
  B You should store them on a cloud server.

Pronunciation
The schwa sound
Go to page 119. 🔊

READING

1 REMEMBER AND CHECK **Answer the questions. Then check your answers in the texts on page 49 in the Student's Book.**

1 What happens when parents try to limit the amount of time their children spend in front of a screen?

2 When did screen time first become an issue?

3 Which city doesn't allow large outdoor advertising any more?

4 What percentage of the population said the ban had improved their quality of life?

5 Give three examples that the text says we use our mobiles for other than making and receiving calls.

6 What have people lost the ability to do?

2 **Read the article quickly. What do these numbers refer to?**

1 234　　　2 2006　　　3 4.7 million

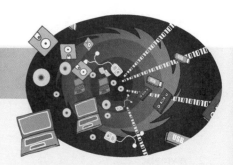

The Digital **Black Hole**

Libraries around the world still hold copies of books printed hundreds of years ago. Will e-books still be accessible to us in hundreds of years' time? Librarians are worried that digital information and digital books are already being lost. Technology is always changing, and even now, we cannot access information typed in programs we used ten or fifteen years ago. Is digital data in danger of disappearing into a digital black hole?

Amazingly, we still have copies of the first published collection of William Shakespeare's 36 plays, *The First Folio*. That's not bad for a book that's nearly 500 years old. The folio was published in 1623. Around 800 copies were printed and 234 known copies still survive today.

More amazingly, there are still copies of the 13th century scientist Al-Jazari's illustrated book on automation and robotics, *The Book of Knowledge of Ingenious Mechanical Devices*. It is thought that Al-Jazari finished writing his book on the 16th January 1206 in Mesopotamia (modern-day Turkey) and copies still survive today.

Books are quite easy to store. They hold a large amount of information in a small space. Most importantly, we don't need any special equipment to open them. But what about the documents stored on your computer now? Will people be able to read them in 800, 500 or even 10 years' time?

Technology moves fast. Documents we saved on floppy discs ten or twenty years ago can't be accessed now. We can't open them on our 21st century laptops. What about all your digital photographs? Every second, thousands of them are uploaded to social media. There is no physical copy. What will happen to them? Will they be lost in a few years' time? Now you save them in .jpg or .tiff format. In ten years' time, there will be another format and another program to open your photos with. This new program will not be able to open your old .jpg or .tiff files. People have recognised this problem and there are now online retailers who will print physical photo albums of your Facebook posts.

Music is in danger of being lost too. We have to think of new ways to store it. The increasing disappearance of the technology to play tapes, vinyl records and even CDs means that millions of music recordings and songs could be lost forever. Archivists must copy this music or find the best way of preserving it for future generations.

When a website closes down, all the information on that website is deleted. It's gone forever. It has disappeared into the 'digital black hole'. Organisations have understood this issue. In 2004, the British Library in the UK started to archive websites that are important culturally and academically for future generations, just like paper-based literature. In 2010, the US Library of Congress signed an agreement with Twitter to archive public Tweets sent by Americans. They have archived all public Tweets sent since the start of Twitter in 2006. That's 400 million Tweets every day!

Wikipedia, the online encyclopedia, holds more than 4.7 million articles. It is the result of over 100 million hours of work. In the event of a digital catastrophe, it could all disappear. The only solution is to print it all out and keep physical copies. In 2014, Pediapress launched a crowdfunding scheme with the aim of raising $50,000 to print Wikipedia as 1,000 books of 1,200 pages each.

With all the amazing new digital technology available to us today, we still have to rely on the centuries-old technology of printing. For now, it seems printed copies are still the safest way to store information.

3 **Read the article again and complete the sentences. Use between 1 and 2 words.**

1 Shakespeare's *First Folio* was published in _____ .

2 Al-Jazari's book about automation and robotics was written at the beginning of the _____ century in _____ .

3 You don't have to have any _____ to open a book.

4 In order to solve the problem of losing your digital photos, you should _____ physical copies of them.

5 We must _____ and public Tweets for future generations.

6 Even though we have lots of amazing new technology, _____ are still the most secure way to save information.

DEVELOPING WRITING

A guide to buying a phone

1 Read Jamie's guide to buying a phone. Circle three things that are important to him.

   A the ringtones   B the battery life   C the pen   D the camera   E the games

---

My Instruction Guide to Buying a New Phone

What do you look for when you buy a phone? Does your phone have to be the latest model? Does it have to look good or do you just want a phone that's easy to use and small enough to fit in your pocket? Before you buy your new phone, decide what's important to you.

First I look at the battery life of a phone. That's very important to me. It must have a long battery life. It mustn't ever go flat on me. Next I look at the camera quality. I like taking photos so I have to have a phone with a good camera. I also like to have a phone with a big screen so I can see the photos clearly. Then I look at how easy it is to do things, for example adding a name to my contacts, finding someone in my contacts, sending a text message to multiple people, using the autocorrect and sending a photo. After that I check the games. What are they like? Finally, I look at the price of the phone. Is it affordable? I do that last but my mum says I should do it first!

Everyone has different priorities when buying a phone, but these are the things that are important to me.

---

2 Read Jamie's guide again and underline the sequencing words. Then complete the list of sequencing words.

First

_____

Then

_____

Finally

3 You are going to write your own guide to buying (a) a new phone or (b) a tablet or (c) a laptop. First brainstorm your ideas and complete the mind map.

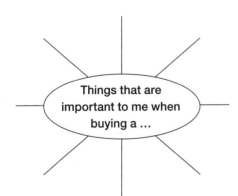

Things that are important to me when buying a …

4 Now pick five of those ideas and write them in sequence using the terms below.

First

Next

Then

After that

Finally

5 Now write your own guide to buying a new phone, tablet or laptop in 200–250 words.

CHECKLIST

- [ ] Include modal verbs in your guide
- [ ] Include a variety of useful technology nouns and verbs
- [ ] The information in your guide is in a logical order (the most important feature first, the least important last)
- [ ] Use sequencing words

LISTENING

1 🔊 17 **Listen to the conversation between Matt, Alicia and Oscar and circle the correct option.**

1 Alicia spends a lot of time playing *tennis* / *video games*.

2 Alicia *texts* / *sees* her friends all the time.

3 When Jo called Matt, she was *excited* / *upset*.

2 🔊 17 **Listen again and answer the questions.**

1 What do Matt, Alicia and Oscar have to do for homework?

_____

2 Why doesn't Alicia want to let her mum see their homework?

_____

3 What should Alicia stop doing?

_____

4 What does Oscar suggest Alicia should do?

_____

5 What is Alicia looking forward to hearing about?

_____

6 Why was Jo upset?

_____

3 🔊 17 **Listen again and complete these parts of the conversation.**

1 **MATT** What do you think of the homework? I can't believe Mr Harrow _____ this thing.

ALICIA You mean the video gaming guide for parents? I think it's OK. Mind you, I'm not going to show it to my mum. She's already worried about me spending too much time playing video games. She _____ during the week at all.

OSCAR You do spend a lot of time on the games console, Alicia. You _____ more.

2 **ALICIA** What do you mean?

MATT You know what he means. You just sit around staring at screens all day.

OSCAR You're turning into a couch potato. You _____ some exercise.

3 **JO** Hi, Alicia. I haven't heard from you for ages.

ALICIA I know, I'm sorry. Listen. Matt, Oscar and I are going to Bob's Café. Would you like to come along? We can't wait to hear about your skiing trip.

JO I'd love to come. I'll meet you all there in an hour.

ALICIA Great. We'll see you there. Oh, and you _____ any money – it's on me!

DIALOGUE

1 **Complete the dialogues with the phrases in the list.**

need to finish | had better get | made me
have to help me | should leave | make me do it

1

MARIA Hi, Susie. How did your audition go yesterday?

SUSIE I don't think I'll get a part in the school play.

MARIA How come?

SUSIE I made a mess of the audition. I couldn't remember my lines. It was awful. Then they _____ sing. And that was worse. You know I can't sing in tune.

2

JAKE You _____ with the washing up, Sarah. Mum told you to.

SARAH I can't. I'm busy. I _____ this essay.

JAKE You're always busy. You never do anything around the house.

SARAH Oh, no. Here we go.

JAKE You're always on your phone or on your laptop. I always have to do the washing up. It's not fair.

SARAH You can't _____, Jake.

JAKE No, I can't, but Mum can and she's just come home now.

3

ANTONIO What's the matter with you?

JOE I'm just tired. That's all.

ANTONIO Why are you so tired?

JOE I'm not sure. Mind you, I did go to sleep really late last night. I started browsing the Internet and I couldn't stop.

ANTONIO That explains it then. You _____ some sleep now. And you _____ your phone in the living room at night. If it's not in your bedroom, you won't be able to go online. Problem solved.

2 **Now write a dialogue of between six and eight lines. Complain to a friend that he/she is spending too much time in front of a screen. Give him/her some advice. Include some of the words below.**

should / shouldn't | need to | let | make
have to / don't have to | must / mustn't | had better

Reading and Use of English part 7

1 **You are going to read an advertisement for four different tech courses. For questions 1–10, choose from the courses (A–D). The courses may be chosen more than once.**

On this course …

1 you have to work with a small group of people. ☐

2 the main focus will be Hypertext Markup Language. ☐

3 you have to have some artistic and creative ability. ☐

4 you will learn the necessary skills to get a job with a digital company. ☐

5 you will learn the basics of web development. ☐

6 the first thing you do is learn to draw on a computer. ☐

7 you must face new challenges each day. ☐

8 there is time away from the screens to participate in activities outside. ☐

9 you will leave with the skills to develop you own web pages. ☐

10 there will be competitions so students can test their skills. ☐

Tech Heaven ■

Courses for the digital age

Course A: Animation ▰▰▰▰▰▰▰▰

This course is for creative people who like to draw. You don't have to have amazing drawing skills but you need to have some artistic talent. You start learning how to draw on the computer and you finish by making interactive films. You work very closely with teachers to learn the essential techniques. You choose to do either game design or an animation. There is a huge gaming library at the camp so you will have the opportunity to test your gaming skills against other students in our gaming tournaments.

Course B: Web ▰▰▰▰▰▰▰▰

This course is for teens who want to create their own web pages and websites. On this course, you will learn the foundations of web development. The primary focus of the course is HTML, which makes up the building blocks of the Internet. You will leave the camp with your own web page and you will be able to go home and create other web pages.

Course C: Coding ▰▰▰▰▰▰▰▰

This course is ideal for students with some programming experience who want to improve their coding skills. Most devices, programs, computers and robots run on software applications so you must have programming, scripting and coding skills to get a job with a digital company. You will learn from experienced and supportive staff and you will leave the school equipped with the basic skills. There are two hours of outdoor sports activities a day to get some fresh air.

Course D: Robotics ▰▰▰▰▰▰▰▰

This course is all about robots. You will work in small teams and learn how to use VEX® Robotics Design System. You'll build a robot that will compete in robo-football and obstacle courses. You will learn how to build robotic arms and advanced sensors. Every day will present you with a new challenge and every day will be more fun and more inspiring than the last.

GRAMMAR

Comparatives SB page 58

1 ★☆☆ Look at the website and mark the sentences T (true) or F (false).

	JOURNEY TIME	PRICE	COMFORT	FREQUENCY	NUMBER OF PASSENGERS PER WEEK	OVERALL EXPERIENCE
www.travelcompare.com – **London – Paris**						
Euroair	50m	£350	*****	Mon, Tues and Fri	200	*****
Budgetline	1h 15m	£21	*	Wed, Fri and Sat	200	*

1 Euroair is not nearly as quick as Budgetline. ☐

2 Budgetline is far more frequent than Euroair. ☐

3 Budgetline is not nearly as good as Euroair. ☐

4 Budgetline is much cheaper than Euroair. ☐

5 Euroair is much more unpopular than Budgetline. ☐

6 Budgetline is a lot slower than Euroair. ☐

7 Euroair is much better than Budgetline. ☐

8 Budgetline is nowhere near as expensive as Euroair. ☐

2 ★★★ Look at the website in Exercise 1 again and use the words in brackets to make sentences about the London to Paris flights.

0 (nowhere near / comfortable)

Budgetline is nowhere near as comfortable as Euroair.

1 (much / expensive)

_____

2 (just as / popular)

_____

3 (far / quick)

_____

4 (nowhere near / good)

_____

5 (just as / frequent)

_____

6 (not nearly / cheap)

_____

3 ★★☆ Use a ' … and …' expression and the adjective in brackets to rewrite each sentence.

0 The boys just won't stop growing. (tall)

The boys are growing taller and taller.

1 Every year there are more cars on the road. (busy)

_____

2 I love spring. Every day the sun stays up a few minutes later. (long)

_____

3 Scientists say the temperature of the Earth is increasing. (hot)

_____

4 The price of food is increasing by the week. (expensive)

_____

4 ★★★ Use a 'the …, the …' comparative expression to rewrite each sentence.

0 Loud music gives me a bad headache.

The louder the music gets, the worse my headache gets.

1 Hot weather makes me angry.

_____

2 Driving fast is dangerous.

_____

3 When you're hungry, food tastes better.

_____

4 Old people need less sleep.

_____

Linkers of contrast SB page 61

5 ★☆☆ **Match the sentence halves.**

1 Although not many people came to the party, ☐
2 I feel really tired today ☐
3 Liam invited Dan to his party ☐
4 In spite of having sold millions of books, ☐
5 The film was in French so I didn't understand much. ☐
6 The athlete wasn't 100% fit. ☐

a even though they're not the best of friends.
b no one knows who she is.
c However, I still really enjoyed it.
d Nevertheless, she still won the race easily.
e we still had a great time.
f despite having had a really good night's sleep.

6 ★★☆ **Complete the card with the missing linkers.**

¹A _ _ _ _ ou _ _ you annoy me at least once a day.
²I _ _ _ _ i _ e o _ the fact you always get your way.
³E _ e _ _ _ _ ou _ _ you take things without saying 'please'.
And ⁴ _ e _ _ i _ e the mess in my room that you leave.
It seems I don't like you.
⁵ _ e _ e _ _ _ e _ e _ _ _,
that's not true.
There's something I need to say about you.
It seems we're so different. ⁶ _ o _ e _ e _ _,
we're not.
You are my sister – the best friend that I've got.

7 ★★★ **Combine the two sentences using the word in brackets.**

Unusual facts about me

0 I'm short. I'm good at basketball. (despite)
   Despite being short, I'm good at basketball.
1 I've got two bikes. I can't ride a bike. (although)
   _____
2 My mum's French. I don't speak French. (however)
   _____
3 I love Italian food. I don't like pizza. (even though)
   _____
4 I always go to bed early. I'm always late for school. (nevertheless)
   _____
5 I'm 1.75m tall. I'm only 14. (in spite of)
   _____

GET IT RIGHT! 👁

however

Learners often use *however* incorrectly.

✓ *I looked back in his direction.* **However,** *he had vanished.*

✗ *I looked back in his direction* ~~however~~, *he had vanished.*

Match the sentences, then rewrite them using *however.*

0 Tom asked Helen out. [a]
   Tom asked Helen out. However, she said no.
1 Ethan was offered the position of school counsellor. ☐
   _____
2 Loom bands used to be a big craze. ☐
   _____
3 The passengers were stuck on the train for two hours. ☐
   _____
4 The Ice Bucket Challenge raised awareness about ALS. ☐
   _____
5 President Obama refused to do the challenge. ☐
   _____

a She said no.
b Nobody spoke to each other.
c He turned it down.
d He donated money instead.
e It also wasted a lot of water.
f It seems to be over now.

VOCABULARY

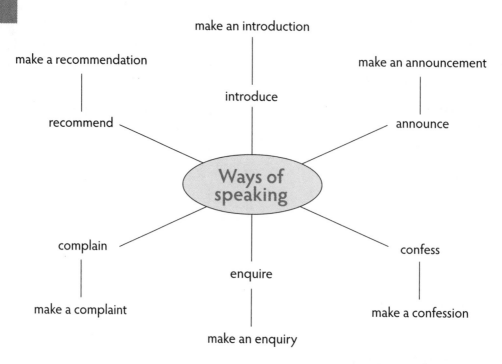

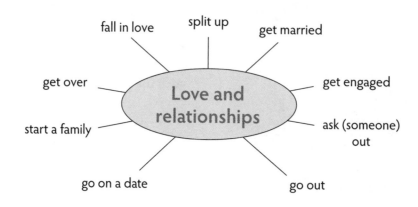

Key words in context

craze	In 2014 loom bands were a huge **craze** all over the planet.
dreaded	My **dreaded** piano exam is next week. I'm not looking forward to it at all.
go viral	The video of his cat playing the piano **went viral**. People were watching it all over the world.
groan	The children **groaned** when the teacher told them he was giving them a surprise test.
in their stride	When the plane was delayed by 4 hours most people took it **in their stride** and didn't complain (though of course a few were unhappy).
nominate	I'd like to **nominate** Luca for class president.
participant	The **participants** in this quiz show can win up to £100,000.
sufferer	Doctors say there will soon be a new medicine to help allergy **sufferers**.
sweep	Every year dozens of hurricanes **sweep** through the area.

Ways of speaking SB page 58

1 ★☆☆ **Unscramble the verbs and then match them to the nouns.**

verb

1 edomrcnme _____ ☐
2 nosecfs _____ ☐
3 toridnceu _____ ☐
4 reuqeni _____ ☐
5 nnoanuec _____ ☐
6 icmnlaop _____ ☐

noun (to make a/an …)

a enquiry
b confession
c announcement
d complaint
e recommendation
f introduction

2 ★★☆ **Circle the correct option.**

1 'What time does the train leave?'
Making a/an *confession / introduction / enquiry*

2 'This fish isn't cooked properly.'
Making a/an *complaint / introduction / announcement*

3 'The library will close in half an hour.'
Making a/an *confession / recommendation / announcement*

4 'You should try the pepperoni pizza. It's excellent.'
Making a/an *enquiry / recommendation / complaint*

5 'Harry, I'd like you to meet Tom.'
Making a/an *introduction / announcement / enquiry*

6 'I'm really sorry, it was me who broke the computer.'
Making a *complaint / confession / recommendation*

3 ★★☆ **Complete the sentences with the missing verbs.**

1 'OK, it was me. I ate the last piece of cake,' she
_____ .

2 'Can you tell me what time the shop closes?' she
_____ .

3 'The Internet isn't working in my room,' she
_____ to the hotel manager.

4 'You should read this book, it's great,' he
_____ .

5 He _____ me to Ian. 'Ian, this is Dan. Dan, this is Ian.'

6 'I've got a new job,' he _____ to the whole room.

Love and relationships SB page 59

4 ★☆☆ **Circle the correct words.**

1 Sometimes I think I'll never fall *on / in* love.

2 Have you heard? Deb and Dexter have *started / split* up.

3 We got *married / engaged* in a church.

4 Bob just proposed to me and I said 'yes'. I can't believe it. I'm *engaged / married*.

5 I really want to ask Jim *out / up* but I'm too scared.

6 Harry and Bella have been *going / asking* out together for half a year already.

7 My brother's going *on / off* a date tonight. He's so nervous.

8 They've only just got married so I don't think they'll want to *get / start* a family soon.

9 Liam is still in love with Jessica. I don't think he'll ever get *up with / over* her.

5 ★★☆ **Put the events in order.**

☐ He said 'yes' and they agreed to go on a date.

☐ Apparently they're already thinking of starting a family.

☐ 1 Olivia split up with Mike.

☐ It didn't take them long to fall in love.

☐ They got married a few weeks ago.

☐ It took him a long time to get over it.

☐ And six months later they got engaged.

☐ Eventually Lucy, his friend's sister, asked him out.

☐ It was a success and they started going out together.

READING

1 REMEMBER AND CHECK Read the article on page 60 of the Student's Book again. Write down the significance of these numbers.

0 2014   *The year the ice-bucket challenge happened.*

1 $10   _____

2 $100   _____

3 24   _____

4 2   _____

5 2.5 million   _____

6 150   _____

7 15%   _____

8 10%   _____

2 Read the two stories. Make a list of all the things they have got in common.

The kindness of strangers

When Katie Cutler heard about an attack on 67-year-old Alan Barnes, she immediately knew what she had to do, even though she had never met him.

Alan had been mugged outside his home in Gateshead in the North East of England. He had been pushed to the ground by a man demanding money, who then ran off after Alan cried for help. For Alan, who has problems with his eyesight and is only 1.37m tall, the attack was terrifying and he felt reluctant to return back home alone.

When the story made the news, Katie immediately set up a page on a fundraising website called *Go Fund Me* with the intention of making £500 to help Alan find a new house to rent. The story went viral on the Internet and was picked up by most TV news stations. Less than a week after the fund was started Katie had raised £284,000 with donations from 21,700 people. With people making donations from the UK, Canada, the Netherlands and other countries, it was truly an international response.

Alan had the chance to thank Katie in person when the two finally met. He told her that he planned to use the money to buy a home of his own and several local builders had also offered to help make sure that Alan's new house was in perfect condition, and what he deserved.

Glenn Buratti had a disappointing turnout for his birthday party to celebrate his 6th birthday. Despite having invited all the children from his class, not one of them turned up at his house in Florida, USA on the day.

Glenn, who suffers from mild autism and epilepsy, was so upset that his mother Ashley decided to share her frustration on Facebook. She posted a message in which she told of the situation and the sadness she felt seeing the disappointment of her son.

It wasn't long before the online community was in touch and within minutes many people had got in contact asking if they could bring their children over. But it wasn't just children who came, the news also reached the local sheriff's office, which sent a helicopter to fly over his house to the young boy's delight.

A few days later a surprised Glenn received a visit at home from the county police and fire services, who had come to wish him a happy birthday and gave the happy boy a tour of their many vehicles. Glenn also became an Internet star with his story going viral and being featured in newspapers and TV news stations all over the world.

3 Read the stories again. Who might have said these things (and to whom)?

	Who said it?	… to whom?
1 Why is there no one here?		
2 I can't wait to move.		
3 Look. The pilot's waving at you.		
4 When I started this I could never have imagined how generous people could be.		
5 Thank you. You've changed my life.		
6 Leave me alone.		
7 Why is there a fire engine outside our house?		
8 Why didn't you just tell me you weren't coming?		

4 Choose two of the characters from either story and write a short (8 line) dialogue between them.

DEVELOPING WRITING

An essay about charity

1 **Read the essay question. Then read the essay and tick the correct summary of the writer's thoughts.**

☐ She believes it's better to donate money.

☐ She believes it's better to donate time.

☐ She believes that all donations are welcome.

> **It's better to donate your time than your money. What do you think?**

When most people hear of a charity asking for a donation they probably wonder how much money they can give. But money's not the only thing you can donate – your time can be just as valuable.

For example, my grandmother spends three afternoons a week volunteering in the local Oxfam shop. One of my friends' fathers spends Monday mornings driving elderly people to their hospital appointments for free. Then there are all those people who donate their lives to helping less fortunate people overseas, doctors and rescue workers who go out to help when earthquakes hit, for example. Of course, they get paid a little, but nowhere near as much as they could earn doing their jobs at home.

If you've got spare money, then making a donation is not too much trouble. You simply drop some coins in a collection box, buy items from charity organisations or make online payments. It never takes more than a few minutes. Giving away your time for free is different and it shows real dedication to the charity.

Charities rely on the kindness of people and without them, the good work that they do would not get done. Whether it be your time or your money, most charities are always happy to accept either.

> ### Writing tip: using examples
>
> - You can often make your essays more accessible to the reader by including some real examples from everyday life. This will help the reader relate more easily to what you are saying. For example, this essay is all about charitable donations, both of money and time. The reader has included examples of both.
>   e.g: Time: grandmother helping in local charity shop.
>   Money: put money in a collection box.
> - This is not only a good chance to help you engage your reader, but it can also give you the chance to show your range of vocabulary. It will also help with your organisation too.

2 **Look back at the essay and find two more examples from real life of:**

How people donate their time:

_____

_____

How people donate their money:

_____

_____

3 **Write down three more ways that people can donate their time to charity.**

1 _____

2 _____

3 _____

4 **Now write your answer to the essay question in around 200 words.**

CHECKLIST

☐ Include good examples from everyday life

☐ Make your opinion clear in the last paragraph

☐ Make sure you answer the question asked

☐ Try and show a good range of vocabulary

LISTENING

1 🔊 18 Listen to three conversations Ava has during her journey to Scotland. Order the pictures.

2 🔊 18 Listen again and answer the questions.

CONVERSATION 1

1 How much cheaper is the later train?

2 What time train does Ava get?

CONVERSATION 2

3 What three items does Ava choose?

4 How much more expensive is a large juice?

CONVERSATION 3

5 How long is Ava staying in Glasgow?

6 How long is Ava staying on the Isle of Mull?

3 🔊 18 Complete the sentences from the conversations, then listen again and check.

CONVERSATION 1

TICKET OFFICER If you can wait an hour and get the 9.55 it's a w_____ l_____ cheaper.

AVA Yes, that's a much better idea b_____ f_____.

CONVERSATION 2

ASSISTANT It's e_____ the best deal for you.

ASSISTANT And it's e_____ cheaper if you've got a Trainclub card.

CONVERSATION 3

PASSENGER Mull's f_____ and a_____ more spectacular than the Lake District.

PASSENGER It's smaller and m_____ less crowded.

DIALOGUE

1 Put the dialogue in order.

	DAD	It's a ten minute walk!
	DAD	You know what? I've got a good idea. You drive the kids in the car, or taxi or whatever. I'll take the train and we'll all meet on the beach.
	DAD	No chance, I thought we'd make it a tech free day too. Just a good old family day out on the train.
	DAD	I thought we'd go to Prestatyn. It's by far a nicer beach.
1	DAD	Who fancies a day at the beach?
5	DAD	I said how about a beach day, not a shopping day. Tim, how about you?
	DAD	I'm not. It's a whole lot easier than taking the car. And the train's quicker too. It's easily the best option.
13	MUM	We'll probably miss the train and have to wait hours for the next one.
	MUM	That sounds like a great idea. Shall we go to Llandudno?
	MUM	Well, I'm not so sure. I think I agree with the kids on this one. It's miles more convenient to take the car. I mean we've got to get to the station…
	LUCY	But Llandudno's got better shops by far.
	LUCY	The train?! Please tell me you're joking.
9	TIM	Yeah, Dad. Please tell us you're joking.
	TIM	Can I take my tablet with me?
	TIM	It'd be even quicker if we took a taxi.

2 Imagine the family are on the beach. They are deciding where to eat lunch. Write a 10 line dialogue. Try and use some comparative structures.

Pronunciation

Linking words with /dʒ/ and /tʃ/
Go to page 119. 🔊

Reading and Use of English part 7

You are going to read an article about four teenagers talking about how they use social media. For questions 1–10, choose from the teenagers (A–D). The teenagers may be used more than once.

Which teenager …

1 likes to post photos on social media?

2 thinks it's more popular with the older generation?

3 has phases when they use social media more?

4 uses social media less than they did before?

5 gave up using social media because of a bad experience?

6 uses social media to let their friends know a lot of the things that are happening in their life?

7 likes to use social media for practical things?

8 doesn't think their life is interesting enough to write about it on social media?

9 thinks people hide their true emotions on social media?

10 uses social media to feel closer to friends they don't see every day?

A Gabby

I have a strange relationship with social media. I can go for months without using it and then I'll spend a week or so posting stuff on my wall every half an hour. Then someone will write something horrible on it and I'll stop using it again for a while. I think when I'm generally happy I don't feel the need to use it but when I'm not quite so happy it makes me feel better if I do use it. It's funny really, everyone on social media always seems so happy but I'm sure they aren't. They're probably just like me – pretending to be. I helped my mum set up an account the other day. It was funny to see how excited she got with this 'new' technology. Anyway, in a couple of days she had over 200 friends. I think she's more popular than me.

B Andy

I used to be a massive fan of social media but these days I don't use it nearly as much as I used to. To be honest, I think it's something that appeals more to old people like my parents. They think it's a brilliant way of getting back in touch with people they haven't seen for years. It's different to my situation. I see most of my friends every day so I don't really need it to keep in touch. I do use it, however, for organising things. I play football on Sunday mornings so every Saturday evening I send out a message to see who wants to play and to check if we've got enough players. It's really useful for that sort of thing. I also use it sometimes if I want to get in contact with just one person privately. It's good for that but I don't really feel the need to share my life online.

C Carmen

I never really use social media. It's not that I'm against it, it's just that I don't really have the time. I'm too busy with my day-to-day life, school work, piano lessons, dance classes. I just don't really have the time to sit down and let people know what's happening in my life and I'm sure they'd find it really boring if I did. Mine isn't the most exciting life. Besides, I see all my best friends every day so I can let them know what's happening face-to-face. It's a lot quicker. But I wasn't always like this. When I first got my phone about three years ago I used to spend hours updating my Facebook page, but then I started to get some nasty comments on my wall. They were pretty upsetting and I found the best way to stop this happening was to not use social media. To be honest I don't really miss it much.

D Mike

I love social media. I use it all the time. I must write at least eight posts a day on my wall. I've got friends in quite a few different places and I think it's the perfect way of keeping in touch with everyone and letting them know what's going on in my life – it doesn't have to just be the big things, I think it's important to share the small things too, like a good book you've read, a photo of a delicious meal and so on. I know some people think it's a bit silly to share so much of your life but I think if you've got good friends, they're interested in hearing these things. It's great to see their comments too. It makes you feel like you're actually with them and you don't miss them so much. I also message friends individually when I've got something more personal to say. But I don't do this so often.

CONSOLIDATION

LISTENING

1 🔊20 **Listen to Sam saying how she met her husband Jim and answer the questions.**

1 What instrument did Jim play in the band?

_____

2 How many members were there in the band?

_____

3 Where did Sam work?

_____

4 When did Sam tell Jim that she'd seen him before in his band?

_____

2 🔊20 **Listen again and mark the sentences T (true) or F (false).**

1 Jim's band had some local support. ☐

2 Jim always played his trumpet at the front of the stage. ☐

3 Sam tried to meet Jim when he was in a band. ☐

4 Jim left the band after a year. ☐

5 Sam was Jim's boss at the theatre. ☐

6 Sam kept her secret from Jim until they were married. ☐

GRAMMAR

3 **Match the sentence halves.**

1 You had better leave soon ☐

2 You're supposed to arrive before 9 am ☐

3 The test was really difficult ☐

4 There was a lot of traffic ☐

5 The more I listen to the new Kaiser Chiefs album, ☐

6 Dad says it's getting more ☐

7 Even though I didn't know anyone there, ☐

8 In spite of really studying hard, ☐

a but somehow I managed to pass.

b and we were only just able to get to the airport in time.

c and more difficult to find parking in the city centre.

d I failed the test badly.

e if you don't want to get a 'late' mark.

f I still really enjoyed the party.

g if you don't want to miss the train.

h the more I like it.

VOCABULARY

4 **Complete the missing words.**

1 To c_____ to the Internet you need a w_____ r_____.

2 To p_____ your laptop in you need a p_____ l_____ and an a_____ (if you're in a foreign country).

3 If you want to do video conferencing you need a w_____ and maybe a h_____.

4 To keep your phone safe you should use a p_____ c_____.

5 To connect your keyboard to your computer you might use a U_____ p_____.

6 If your laptop is out of power you will need to use the c_____.

7 If your computer is slow when you b_____ the Internet, you need to u_____ your system.

8 This software lets you s_____ your laptop and your phone so they're always up-to-date with each other.

5 **Use one word from each list to complete the reported statements. There are two extra words in each list.**

recommended | confessed | enquired
introduced | announced | complained

out with | engaged | in love with
up with | on a date | a family

1 'We're expecting our first baby in May.'

She _____ that they were starting

_____.

2 'You really should go to the cinema with George. You'll really like him.'

He _____ going _____ with George.

3 'Are Sue and Mike a couple?'

He _____ whether Sue was going _____ Mike.

4 'I can't hide my feelings any longer. I'm mad about you.'

She _____ that she was falling _____ me.

DIALOGUE

6 Put the dialogue in order.

	OLIVIA	No, I'm tired of doing that. They never fix it properly. It's time for a new one.
	OLIVIA	What! Today is Monday. I'm not waiting five days. I'm off to the shops. Now!
	OLIVIA	Not if they don't fix it properly. It will just be a waste of my time.
	OLIVIA	You always say that but then you never do.
	OLIVIA	I don't know. I was trying to save a document and the whole computer crashed.
1	OLIVIA	I don't believe it. My laptop's broken again.
	LIAM	It sounds serious. You'd better take it to the repair shop.
	LIAM	Well I will this time. I promise. I'll take a look at it over the weekend.
	LIAM	Again? What is it this time?
	LIAM	What! It will be miles cheaper to get it fixed. It's the best solution by far.
	LIAM	Well at least let me have a look at it first. Maybe I can fix it.

READING

7 Read the article and put the events in order.

- [ ] He connects the hose pipe with the toilet.
- [ ] The boy is presented with a bill to pay.
- [ ] He asks the club for help.
- [ ] The boy is fishing on a lake with his friends.
- [ ] He loses his phone.
- [ ] The police question the boy about his actions.
- [ ] The club owner arrives.
- [ ] Water pours into the club.
- [ ] He arrives at the club with equipment to help him find his phone.

WRITING

8 Write a paragraph of about 120 words about an occasion when you had a problem with technology. Include:

- what the problem was
- how it affected you
- what you did to try and solve the problem

Desperate measures

The amount of time that teenagers spend in front of a screen is a huge concern for many parents all over the world. But are they worrying unnecessarily? After all, didn't their parents worry about how much time they spent in front of the TV every day? Aren't computers just the modern-day equivalent of the television or is it more than that? Many experts seem to think that many teenagers are actually addicted to technology and would find it very difficult to spend a day without it. The parents of one 16-year-old boy in Germany may have agreed with them when they found out just how far their son would go for his mobile phone.

The boy was on a fishing trip in a boat on a small lake with his friends when his phone slipped out of his hand and fell into the water – gone forever, so it would seem. But the boy refused to accept that that would be the last he would ever see of it. Even though he knew that the phone itself would be ruined, he was determined to retrieve the data card it contained with all his contact information and photos on it. This information was far too important to lose, and so he started to think what he could do to find the phone.

His first plan involved asking the fishing club, who owned the lake, if he could borrow a diving suit so he could jump into the water and search for the phone. Unsurprisingly they decided he couldn't and advised him to give up trying to find his phone. It was then he realised this was something he was going to have to do on his own when no one was watching. So later that night he went back to the lake with two water pumps and some hose pipes. His idea was simple. He was going to drain all the water out of the lake and find his phone lying at the bottom.

He decided that the best place to pump the water into would be the club's toilet. He managed to connect one end of the pipe to the pump and put the other end into the toilet. However, what he didn't know was that the toilet was connected to a small tank rather than a larger sewer system. The result was that the tank was quickly filled up and the water started to flood into the club car park. The boy tried to stop the flow but the more he tried, the worse the situation got and before he knew it there was water everywhere. When the club owner arrived he immediately called the police, leaving the boy with a lot of explaining to do. Sadly the boy was unable to find his phone. All he got was a big bill for the cost of cleaning up the mess he had created.

7 ALWAYS LOOK ON THE BRIGHT SIDE

GRAMMAR

Ways of referring to the future (review)

SB page 68

1 ★☆☆ **Write sentences with the correct future form of the verbs.**

0   I / play / tennis / with Milly / tomorrow
    I'm playing tennis with Milly tomorrow.

1   My dad / go / to / Berlin / on business / next month
    _____

2   The / lesson / start / in / ten minutes
    _____

3   As soon as / Mum / get / home / we / go / to / the cinema
    _____

4   We / not have dinner / until / Dad / come / home
    _____

5   Tina and Tom / stay / with / their aunt / in / Mexico / in / the summer holidays
    _____

2 ★★☆ **Complete the dialogue with the correct form of the verbs. Use the present continuous or *going to*.**

SALLY   0 *Are you coming* (you / come) on the school trip this summer?

NATHAN   I'm not sure. I [1]_____ (ask) my parents this evening.

SALLY   Matt and Lucy [2]_____ (not plan) to come. They [3]_____ (travel) overland to Turkey with their family this summer.

NATHAN   That sounds exciting.

SALLY   Yes, they [4]_____ (drive) across France, Switzerland and Italy. Then they [5]_____ (take) a car ferry from Italy to Turkey, via Greece.

NATHAN   Awesome! When [6]_____ (Mr Jones / hold) the meeting about the school trip?

SALLY   He [7]_____ (organise) it for next Saturday at 2 pm.

3 ★★☆ **Complete the mini-dialogues with the correct future form of the verbs in brackets.**

1   A   What _____ (you / do) on Saturday?
    B   I _____ (go) to a craft fair with my sister.

2   A   Do you think your mum _____ (let) you come and stay for the weekend?
    B   Yes, I think so. I _____ (ask) her tonight.

3   A   What time _____ (the football match / start) on Saturday?
    B   It _____ (start) at two o'clock.

4   A   I _____ (look for) a Saturday job. I'd like to work in a clothes shop.
    B   Really? My brother and I _____ (join) a climbing club so I can't get a Saturday job.

5   A   It's my birthday tomorrow. I hope it _____ (be) sunny because we _____ (have) a barbecue in the afternoon!
    B   I don't think it _____ (rain) tomorrow. The weather's been so nice today.

6   A   What time _____ (the train / leave)?
    B   It _____ (leave) at six o'clock.

4 ★★☆ **Will it happen or won't it happen? What do you think? Read the notes and write sentences.**

0   Scientists (build) a lift into space.
    Scientists won't build a lift into space.

1   Your computer (have) a sense of smell.
    _____

2   Facebook still (be) the biggest social network.
    _____

3   Robots (do) all the work on farms.
    _____

4   Planes (fly) without pilots.
    _____

5   We (be able to) upload the contents of our brains to our computers.
    _____

6   People (be able to) touch each other through their phones.
    _____

Future continuous and future perfect
SB page 69

5 ★☆☆ **Write sentences in the future continuous.**

The holiday's finally here. I'm so excited. This time tomorrow …

1 I / swim / in the sea

_____

2 Sam / look for / shells on the beach

_____

3 Mum / explore / the town

_____

4 Dad / buy / food / at the local market

_____

6 ★★☆ **Complete the mini-dialogues with the verbs in the future perfect tense.**

1 A We're late. They _____ everything by the time we get there. (eat)

B I'm sure they _____ something for us. (leave)

2 A Hi, Miriam. I thought you were coming round to my house this afternoon. Everybody's here.

B I am coming. I'll be there at six.

A But everybody _____ home by then. (go)

3 A Are you looking forward to the charity swimming event tomorrow?

B Yes. By this time tomorrow, we _____ across the Bosphorus from Asia to Europe. (swim)

4 A Have you got any plans for the future?

B Yes. By the time I'm thirty, I _____ around the world. (travel)

7 ★★☆ **Choose the correct option to complete the mini-dialogues.**

1 A Dad's plane lands at eight o'clock.

B It's 8.30 now. His plane _will be landing / will have landed_.

2 A Hey, you're going to the Lake District this weekend, right?

B Yes, by this time on Saturday, I _will be sailing / will sail_ across Lake Windermere.

3 A By the time I'm fifty, they _will be finding / will have found_ a cure for cancer. I'm sure.

B I hope so.

4 A The show starts at 7 pm.

B Then I'm sorry, I can't come. I _will be eating / will eat_ dinner with my family at that time.

5 A Mum, I'm going round to Matt's house.

B What about your homework?

A I _will have done / will do_ it later.

8 ★★☆ **Complete the email with the phrases in the list.**

'll be having | 'll send | 'll have been shopping
'll be | 'll be going | 'll have seen | 'll text
'll be staying | 'll have visited

Hey Lily,

Well, this time tomorrow, I ¹_____ in London. How cool is that! We ²_____ at a hotel on the South Bank. I Googled it and it's near the Globe Theatre. I ³_____ you a photo when we get there. I know you love anything to do with the theatre and everything about Shakespeare! On the first day, we ⁴_____ to the Tower of London. My mum's keen to see the Crown Jewels. I just want to see the ravens and the Beefeaters, of course. Oh, yes! And guess what? We ⁵_____ lunch in Speedy's Sandwich Bar and Café on North Gower Street – the one that Benedict Cumberbatch always goes to in the Sherlock Holmes TV series. I can't wait.

So anyway, by the end of the trip, I ⁶_____ the London Dungeons. I ⁷_____ the view from the top of the Shard, and I ⁸_____ at Camden Market. Amazing!

I ⁹_____ you as soon as I get there.

See you soon.

Tanya

GET IT RIGHT!

will

Learners often confuse _would_ and _will_.

✓ _I think it **will** be a good experience._

✗ _I think it would be a good experience._

Complete the sentences with _will_ or _would_.

1 I hope the exam _____ be OK, but to be honest, I'm dreading it.

2 If Dan wasn't such a pessimist, he _____ be much more fun to be with.

3 We're about to go out so I _____ call you later.

4 Thanks for the offer. I _____ be very happy to accept.

5 Sally's really looking forward to visiting us. We _____ have a great time.

6 James is on the point of changing his job. He _____ like to spend less time commuting.

VOCABULARY

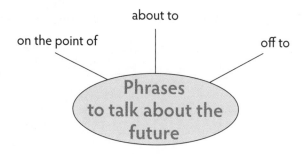

Feelings about future events

Hope for the future
have a really good feeling about
feel quite positive
be really looking forward to

Concerns for the future
dread
just not know where to start
be really worried about
get so worked up about
be a bit unsure about
have a bad feeling about
feel quite apprehensive about

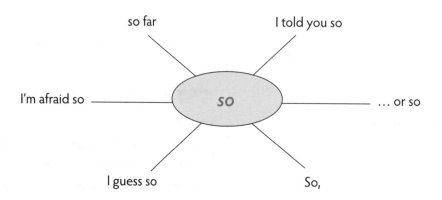

Key words in context

attitude	Kate always thinks good things will happen. She has a very positive **attitude** to life.
cheer (someone) up	My best friend always **cheers me up**. When I'm sad, she makes me feel happy again.
conscious	When he found him at the bottom of the cliff, he was still **conscious**. He could talk to us.
incapable	My friend James is **incapable** of saying anything negative about anybody. He's such a nice person.
inspirational	Steve Jobs made an **inspirational** speech at the 2005 Stanford graduation ceremony.
pessimist	Dan is a terrible **pessimist**. He always thinks something bad will happen.
quote	'All the world's a stage, and all the men and women merely players …' is a **quote** from Shakespeare's play *As You Like It*.
support	My granddad had a lot of **support** from the nurses. They really helped him to get better.
unfortunate	It was **unfortunate** that it rained at my sister's wedding.

Phrases to talk about the future
SB page 68

1 ★☆☆ **Complete with one word.**

1 A Hi, Helen. I was on the p_____ of calling you.
  B Really? That's strange.
2 A I'm o_____ to the cinema. I'll see you later.
  B OK. Enjoy the film.
3 A We're a_____ to have dinner. Would you like to join us?
  B That's OK thanks. I've just eaten.

2 ★★☆ **Match the sentence halves. Then match them to the pictures.**

1 I always feel nervous when I'm about ☐
2 We are on the point of ☐
3 I'm off ☐

a to go to the dentist's.
b to the park. Would you like to come?
c finishing the experiment.

 A ☐  B ☐

 C ☐

3 ★★★ **Write true sentences for you. Include the phrases in brackets.**

1 (about to) _____

_____

2 (on the point of) _____

_____

3 (off to) _____

_____

Feelings about future events
SB page 71

4 ★★☆ **Match the phrases (1–6) with the phrases with similar meaning (a–f).**

1 I'm feeling quite apprehensive. ☐
2 I'm dreading it. ☐
3 I've got a good feeling about it. ☐
4 I'm a bit unsure about it. ☐
5 I'm getting so worked up about it. ☐
6 I just don't know where to start. ☐

a I think it's going to be fine.
b I'm a bit nervous.
c I'm a little uncertain about it.
d I'm not looking forward to it at all.
e I'm not sure what to do first.
f It's really upsetting me.

WordWise
SB page 73

SO

5 ★★☆ **Complete the mini-dialogues with the phrases in the list.**

so far | I told you so | I'm afraid so | or so
I guess so | So

1 A You were right. Sarah will be playing in our team.
  B _____. That's great news.
2 A How many people will be coming on Saturday?
  B I'm not sure. A hundred people have bought tickets _____.
3 A _____, will you be coming to the Science Museum on Monday?
  B I don't know yet. I'll let you know as soon as I can.
4 A Will we all be wearing the same costumes for the show?
  B _____ but I'm not sure.
5 A Do I have to hand my essay in on Tuesday?
  B _____. All essays have to be in by 3 pm Tuesday. That's the final deadline.
6 A I've got to tidy my room by lunchtime.
  B I've got an hour _____ free. I'll help you.

READING

1 REMEMBER AND CHECK **Answer the questions. Then check your answers in the blog on page 67 of the Student's Book.**

1 What does Jim choose to do every day?

_____

2 What did the doctors and nurses in the operating room think when they saw Jim?

_____

3 What did Jim say he was allergic to?

_____

4 What will the writer of the blog choose to find something positive about?

_____

2 Scan the article quickly. What is the significance of each of these numbers? Write a sentence for each.

1 14 _____

2 30 _____

3 2,000 _____

4 300 _____

There is no success without failure

Think of somebody you really admire. Then read their biography. You will probably find that their success didn't come easily. Many famous artists, writers, inventors, sports people, actors and scientists overcame difficulties in their childhood. When the comedian Jim Carrey was fourteen years old, his father lost his job. Jim Carrey took a factory job in the evenings after school to help pay the family's bills.

Sometimes, their success was a surprise, even to themselves. The famous scientist Alexander Fleming said, 'When I woke up just after dawn on 28th September, 1928, I certainly didn't plan to revolutionise all medicine by discovering the world's first antibiotic, or bacteria killer. But I guess that was exactly what I did.'

Another scientist, Thomas Edison, the inventor of the light bulb, believed that every failure was a step towards success. He said, 'If I find 10,000 ways something won't work, I haven't failed. I am not discouraged, because every wrong attempt is another step forward.'

Stephen King, the American author of many horror, science fiction and fantasy books, didn't have immediate success. In fact, he was on the verge of giving up when he finally found success. His first book, *Carrie*, was rejected 30 times and he threw it

into the rubbish bin (no digital copies in those days!). His wife took it out of the bin and encouraged him to send it to other publishers. Finally, it was accepted and it became a huge success. Stephen King went on to sell hundreds of millions of copies of his books.

Some people only become successful after their deaths. The artist Vincent Van Gogh only sold one painting in his lifetime and that was to a friend. Despite this, he kept painting and he painted more than 2,000 artworks in a decade. Now his paintings are very popular and they sell for millions of pounds.

Michael Jordan, the world's most famous basketball player, was rejected by his high school basketball team. He said, 'I can accept failure, everyone fails at something. But I can't accept not trying.' He went on to win the NBA's Most Valuable Player award five times.

One thing all these people have in common is determination to reach their goal no matter what. I leave you with this famous quote from Michael Jordan:

'I've missed more than 9,000 shots in my career. I've lost almost 300 games. 26 times I've been trusted to take the game-winning shot and missed. I've failed over and over and over again in my life and that is why I succeed.'

3 Read the article again. Match the questions (1–6) with the answers (a–f).

1 Who can accept failure but can't accept not trying? ☐

2 Who woke up one morning and discovered something that went on to save millions of people's lives? ☐

3 Who said that every failure was a step towards success? ☐

4 Who worked after school to help buy food for his family? ☐

5 Who only sold one piece of his work in his lifetime? ☐

6 Whose work was rejected thirty times? ☐

a Vincent Van Gogh

b Stephen King

c Michael Jordan

d Jim Carrey

e Alexander Fleming

f Thomas Edison

4 Find another famous author, sports person or singer who failed at first and then succeeded. Write a short paragraph about his/her failure and later success.

DEVELOPING WRITING

A leaflet

1   Quickly read the leaflet and circle the answers.

1   At breakfast, Holly will …
   A   play her favourite song.
   B   sing her favourite song.
   C   listen to her favourite song.
2   Holly will be spending the day …
   A   near a lake.   B   near the sea.   C   up a mountain.
3   She will be watching … in the afternoon.
   A   a play   B   a film   C   the stars
4   The day will end with her friends …
   A   near a lake.   B   in a castle.   C   on a beach.

The Best Day of Your Life

A day designed especially for you!

9.30 am Kick off

When you come down to breakfast, your favourite upbeat 'happy' song will be playing. You will sit down to an amazing breakfast. This will include all your favourite breakfast goodies, and I mean all of them.

Breakfast menu

Cereals with strawberries, hazelnuts and chocolate
Scrambled eggs with mushrooms and toast
A big mug of creamy hot chocolate with a chocolate spoon

10.30 am Vintage Extravaganza

We will be driving to Alnwick Castle on the coast of Northumberland in your favourite sports car – a Jaguar E-type. We'll be at the castle around midday. All your friends will already have arrived.

1 pm Lunch

Lunch will be a barbecue in the castle grounds. Your favourite band, All Directions, will be playing.

2.30 pm Performance of a Lifetime

There will be an open-air performance of your favourite play in the grounds of the castle. And guess who'll be starring in it? Yes, Darcy Night Carol will play the leading role.

8 pm Star Gazing on the Beach

We will be walking to the beach to sit and watch the stars. At around 8.30 pm, we'll be toasting marshmallows on a campfire (your dad will be in charge of that) and looking for your favourite stars.

I know you're going to love it, Holly. Thanks a million for being my best friend.

2   Find synonyms to these words in the leaflet.

1   start   _____
2   positive   _____
3   good things   _____
4   very old   _____
5   outdoor   _____
6   Thank you very much   _____

3   Read the leaflet again and answer the questions.

1   What will Holly be drinking for breakfast?
   _____

2   How will Holly be getting to Alnwick Castle?
   _____

3   What will Holly and her friends be doing for lunch?
   _____

4   Who will be starring in the lead role of the play?
   _____

5   What will Holly and her friends be doing in the evening?
   _____

4   You are going to write a leaflet outlining 'a perfect day' for your best friend. First find out what he/she would most like to do. Write questions to ask your friend.

5   Now you are ready to plan your leaflet. Write notes for each section.

Title
Morning
Afternoon
Evening
Message to your friend

6   Write the leaflet in 200–250 words.

CHECKLIST

☐ The leaflet uses informal language
☐ The language and vocabulary is positive
☐ It is clear and concise
☐ Factual information such as times and places is clearly stated

LISTENING

1 🔊 **21** **Listen and write the numbers of the conversations, 1, 2 or 3 in the boxes.**

a It's about someone who wants to be in the school orchestra. ☐

b It's about someone who wants to be in a band. ☐

c It's about someone who wants to be in the basketball team. ☐

2 🔊 **21** **Listen again and mark the sentences T (true) or F (false).**

CONVERSATION 1

1 Marcus will be playing in the orchestra tonight. ☐

2 May might start piano lessons. ☐

CONVERSATION 2

1 Matt has got a chance of being picked for the team because he's tall. ☐

2 Luckily nobody else wants to be in the basketball team. ☐

CONVERSATION 3

1 Jamie will not be joining the band. ☐

2 Amanda plays the drums really well. ☐

DIALOGUE

1 **Put the dialogue in order.**

☐	SIMON	Don't let it get you down. Your term grades are really good. You were probably just having a bad day.
1	SIMON	Hey, Miranda, cheer up! Things can't be that bad.
☐	SIMON	You see, there is light at the end of the tunnel.
5	SIMON	Hang in there, Miranda. You'll pass it next time.
☐	MIRANDA	Yes, they can. I've failed my Physics exam.
☐	MIRANDA	Thanks, you two. You've really cheered me up.
☐	HELENA	And anyway, you've just got one more year of Physics and then you can give it up.
☐	HELENA	Yes, Simon's right. Look on the bright side, Miranda. You only failed the Physics exam. You could have failed the Chemistry and Maths exams too!

Pronunciation

Intonation: encouraging someone
Go to page 120. 🔊

PHRASES FOR FLUENCY SB page 73

1 **Circle the correct phrases to complete the email.**

⊖ ☐ ✕   ◄ ► ⌂

Hi Kate,

Guess what? I've entered a competition to win a trip to Iceland. My mum warned me not to ¹*go for it / get my hopes up*. Hundreds of people enter competitions like this one. But it's not like I'll ²*make a fool of myself / go for it* or anything. My dad told me to ³*go for it / get my hopes up* anyway. Someone has to win and that someone might be me. Dad's got a very positive attitude to life. ⁴*Fair enough / Anyway*, he's always been successful so he's got nothing to be negative about. But maybe his positivity is the reason for his success. ⁵*Anyway / Fair enough*, I've entered the competition and if I win, I want you to come to Iceland with me. If you don't try, you don't succeed and I've got nothing to lose ⁶*for a start / to make a fool of*.

So fingers crossed we're off to Iceland!

Love

Natalie

2 **Complete these parts of the conversations with the phrases from Exercise 1.**

1 MAY Are you going to tell him?

  GINA No, I don't want to be the one to tell him.

  MAY _____ . I expect Mr Williams will.

2 GINA My piano teacher's really good. You can come and practise with me.

  MAY Why not? I'll _____ .

3 MATT Do you reckon I've got a chance of being in the team? I've got myself really worked up about it.

  HARRY You shouldn't let it get you down like this. Now, I don't want to _____ , but I think you've got a chance.

4 HARRY That's tall! You should get in the team – no problem. However, I know Mike and Jake want to get in the team too.

  MATT Everyone wants to be in the basketball team and there's only one place. I don't want to _____ .

5 PIA Hey, did you hear? Jamie wants to join us.

  JOE Well, he can't, Pia.

  PIA Why not?

  JOE Well, _____ , he can't play any musical instruments.

6 JOE Maybe a few notes. _____ , I've already asked Amanda.

  PIA Asked her what?

Reading and Use of English part 2

1 For questions 1–8, read the text below and think of the word which best fits each gap. Use only one word in each gap. There is an example at the beginning (0).

Top tips for revising

Are you somebody ⁰ _who_ gets very stressed before exams? Well, a little bit of stress is a good thing ¹_____ it encourages you to work hard. However, a lot of stress is not good for you and it can cause tiredness and forgetfulness. This means you won't be at your best ²_____ you take the exam.

Here are five tips to help you cope ³_____ the stress. Firstly, eat healthily. Eat lots of fruit and vegetables and always have a good breakfast before you go to school. Don't eat too many sweets or too ⁴_____ chocolate and don't drink cola or sugary drinks. Secondly, get ⁵_____ of sleep. We recommend eight to ten hours a night. Thirdly, do some exercise. Exercise helps you ⁶_____ relax and gives you more energy, ⁷_____ make sure you include some in your revision timetable. Fourthly, don't leave all your revision until the night before the exam. You won't remember any of it in the morning and you'll feel very tired. Finally, after the exam, don't compare answers with your friends. You've finished the exam and so there is no point worrying about it anymore. Keep busy and enjoy life ⁸_____ you wait to get the results.

Exam guide: open cloze

In this part of the test, there is a cloze text with eight gaps. You must fill the gaps with the correct words to complete the text.

- Read the whole text for general understanding. Remember to give yourself time to read the questions, skim the text, answer the questions, and then check at the end.
- The gaps usually have to be filled with some vocabulary and some grammar words such as relative pronouns, prepositions and auxiliary verbs.
- Think what kind of word is missing. Is it a preposition or is it a linking word or a verb? Look at the words that come immediately before it and after it.
- These are some common kinds of missing words:
  prepositions like *to* and *for*
  linking words like *or* and *but*
  auxiliary verbs like *was* and *will*
  relative pronouns like *that* and *who*
  question words like *what* and *where*
  time expressions like *for*, *ago* and *since*

2 For questions 1–8, read the text below and think of the word which best fits each gap. Use only one word in each gap. There is an example at the beginning (0).

It's sunny so I'm happy

Over the last few decades a lot of research has been done on the relationship ⁰ _between_ mood and weather.

People believe that warm sunny weather cheers people ¹_____. But is this actually true? If you read the international lists of the happiest countries in the world, places like Norway, Sweden, Canada, Denmark and Finland ²_____ always top of the list. They are all countries that have the fewest hours of daylight and sunshine. Indeed, they are not the warmest countries ³_____ the coldest countries. It looks ⁴_____ the opposite is true.

To confirm this theory, the most northerly islands in Scotland – Shetland, Orkney and the Outer Hebrides – have ⁵_____ found to be the happiest region in the whole ⁶_____ the UK. How can this be? It's the coldest region and it only has around 1,000 hours of sunshine a year ⁷_____ to the UK average of 1,340 hours of sunshine. Is it the weather ⁸_____ is it something else that affects your mood? What do you think?

8 MAKING LISTS

GRAMMAR
Conditionals (review) SB page 76

1 ★☆☆ **Match the sentence halves.**

1 I'll put the coffee on ☐
2 If you hadn't been late, ☐
3 If my dad gets up first, ☐
4 I wouldn't post that photo on Facebook ☐
5 If you find the homework difficult, ☐
6 You'd have passed the test ☐
7 If I had the chance, ☐
8 People don't usually go by boat ☐
9 Hannah would be more popular ☐

a if I were you.
b if you'd studied harder.
c I'd go to the USA.
d you'd have seen the beginning of the film.
e if they can afford the air fare.
f if I get up first.
g if she didn't say such nasty things.
h I'll help you.
i he makes breakfast.

2 ★★☆ **Complete the sentences from the prompts.**

0 If we go to Paris, / visit / the Louvre museum.
   If we go to Paris, we'll visit the Louvre museum.

1 If Charles didn't work so much, / have / time / relax
   _____

2 Mark would have taken part in the race if / not break / leg
   _____

3 If people love cats, / often / not like / dogs much
   _____

4 Steve will buy a car if / his father / lend him / money
   _____

5 Ed would ask Jenny out if / not be / so shy
   _____

6 Anne wouldn't have fallen if / see / ice / the path
   _____

3 ★★★ **Complete the gaps with the correct form of the verb given.**

0 If I _had_ (have) more free time, I _would go_ (go) to the cinema more often.

1 If Denise _____ (come) to my party last night, she _____ (meet) my cousin.

2 Sue _____ (put) on weight if she _____ (go on) eating like this.

3 If people _____ (own) a car, they normally _____ (not use) public transport as much.

4 We _____ (visit) our grandmother more often if she _____ (live) closer.

5 If we _____ (see) Peter, we _____ (tell) him you called.

6 You _____ (not fall) off your bike last night if you _____ (not ride) so fast.

7 If James _____ (be) older, he _____ (be able) to see that film.

8 In general, an injection _____ (not hurt) so much if you _____ (relax) completely.

4 ★★★ **Complete the text with the words in the list. There are two you don't need.**

don't │ will │ can't │ hadn't │ won't
had │ 'd have │ would │ had │ wasn't
'd have │ is │ can't │ wouldn't have

Steve is going to do his driving test. His instructor has given him a checklist of things to do when he takes his test. He said, 'Check the car seat. If the seat ¹_____ too far back, you ²_____ find it hard to reach the pedals. And if you ³_____ reach the pedals easily you ⁴_____ drive smoothly. Check the mirrors. If you ⁵_____ look in them, you ⁶_____ see the traffic behind or beside you.' Steve just thought, 'I think I'm going to fail. Not enough lessons. If I ⁷_____ had more time, I ⁸_____ taken more lessons.'

The test was a bit of a disaster. Afterwards he spoke to his instructor. 'If I ⁹_____ remembered to check the mirrors, I ¹⁰_____ driven out into the traffic like I did. I ¹¹_____ passed if I ¹²_____ hit that wall.'

Mixed conditionals `SB page 77`

5 ★★☆ **Write mixed conditional sentences about these situations.**

0 I don't have a big car. I didn't give all my friends a lift to the match.
If I had a big car, I'd have given all my friends a lift to the match.

1 I didn't read his text carefully. Now I don't know where to meet him.

_____

2 Kim didn't see the step. Now she feels really silly.

_____

3 Len arrived very early. Now he's waiting for his friends.

_____

4 I can't help you with your Spanish homework. I didn't study Spanish at university.

_____

5 I left the map at home. I don't know the way to their house.

_____

6 Monica doesn't like opera. She didn't accept Oliver's invitation.

_____

7 Tessa didn't watch the last episode. She doesn't know the ending.

_____

8 Tim is in a hospital bed. He lost control of the car.

_____

6 ★★★ **Complete these mixed conditional sentences. Make them true for you.**

1 If I had _____ last week,
I _____ now.

2 If I hadn't _____ last night,
I wouldn't _____ now.

3 I wouldn't _____ now if I had
_____ last term.

4 I would _____ now if I had
_____ last year.

Pronunciation

Weak forms with conditionals
Go to page 120.

---

7 ★★★ **Look at the pictures and write a conditional sentence for each.**

0 If mum *liked our music, she wouldn't have complained about the noise.*

1 He _____

2 They _____

3 If he _____

GET IT RIGHT! 👁

Conditionals

Learners often use the wrong verb form in conditional clauses.

✓ *I would have remembered if I **had made** a list.*

✗ *I would have remembered if I ~~made~~ a list.*

The underlined parts of the sentences are incorrect. Rewrite the sentences correctly.

1 If the police <u>didn't look</u> into the matter, the crime would never have been discovered.

_____

2 Unless we come up with some new ideas, we <u>wouldn't have</u> a chance of winning the competition.

_____

3 Dave will get the answer as long as we <u>helped</u> him.

_____

4 Suppose I did go to the party, what <u>will</u> I wear?

_____

5 Provided that the calculations were correct, the structure <u>would</u> be totally safe.

_____

6 Come to my house by eight at the latest, otherwise we <u>would</u> miss the beginning of the film.

_____

VOCABULARY

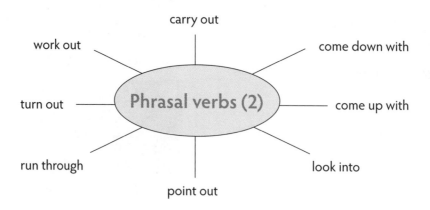

Phrasal verbs (2)

- carry out
- work out
- come down with
- turn out
- come up with
- run through
- look into
- point out

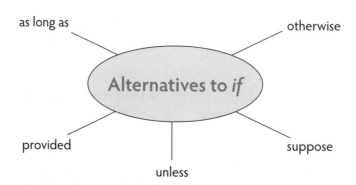

Alternatives to *if*

- as long as
- otherwise
- provided
- suppose
- unless

Key words in context

apparently	That café's always empty – **apparently** the food is really bad there.
calculations	It went wrong because the **calculations** were done badly.
cloth	This jacket isn't hot because it's made of a very light **cloth**.
concrete	The city wasn't beautiful – all the buildings were grey and made of **concrete**.
infection	Wash the cut on your hand right away, to avoid **infection**.
measure	The room is incredibly small – it only **measures** 1.5 metres by 3 metres.
procedure	To make a complaint, you have to fill in a form – that's the **procedure** here.
relevant	That's an interesting story, but it isn't very **relevant** to what we're talking about.
sacred	In India, people don't eat cows because they're **sacred**.
specific	Your back hurts? Please be more **specific** – your lower back or your upper back?
statement	Please answer 'Yes' or 'No' to each **statement** in the questionnaire.
structure	The new bridge is a very beautiful **structure**.

Phrasal verbs (2) SB page 76

1 ★☆☆ **Make a list of eight phrasal verbs from the table. You need to use one of the verbs twice.**

turn come carry look work point run	out through up into down	with

1 _____
2 _____
3 _____
4 _____
5 _____
6 _____
7 _____
8 _____

2 ★★☆ **Rewrite the sentences by replacing the underlined phrase with the correct form of a phrasal verb from Exercise 1.**

0 The strange noises in the night <u>were discovered</u> to be the neighbour's cat.

   The strange noises in the night turned out to be the neighbour's cat.

1 I didn't know where the shop was until Kate <u>showed me</u> the store guide.
_____

2 The instructions for the game were really long, so we just <u>looked at</u> them quickly.
_____

3 The head teacher is <u>investigating</u> the disappearance of the school's pet snake.
_____

4 We couldn't think of what to do until Sally <u>suddenly had</u> a brilliant idea.
_____

5 Janet was having difficulty <u>solving</u> the clues in the crossword.
_____

6 Some volunteers are <u>making</u> repairs to old people's houses.
_____

7 I think we ate something bad – we all <u>got ill with</u> a stomach bug.
_____

3 ★★★ **Write a sentence for a time when you or someone you know …**

1 came down with something.
_____

2 came up with the solution for something.
_____

3 ran through something with someone.
_____

4 worked something out.
_____

5 turned out to be something.
_____

6 carried something out.
_____

Alternatives to *if* SB page 79

4 ★★☆ **Complete the sentences with one of the alternatives to *if*.**

1 We need to take the first train in the morning. _____, we'll be late.

2 _____ Mum heard you say that! She'd be really angry!

3 You can borrow my book _____ you give it back to me tomorrow.

4 Dad said I can't go on the school trip to Russia _____ I buy some travel insurance.

5 You can go there without a visa _____ you don't stay more than three months.

5 ★★★ **Rewrite these sentences using alternatives to *if*. Sometimes there is more than one possibility.**

1 If you didn't live here, where would you like to live?
_____

2 The teacher said I wouldn't do well if I didn't do my homework.
_____

3 OK, you can use my phone if you don't make long-distance calls.
_____

4 I have to go. If I don't, I'll miss the bus.
_____

5 Mum says we can go if we promise to be back in time for dinner.
_____

READING

1 **REMEMBER AND CHECK** Circle the correct options. Then check your answers in the review on page 75 of the Student's Book.

1 A patient got a fever because the doctors didn't wear *gloves / face masks*.

2 Atul Gawande's book is called 'The Checklist Manifesto: How to *avoid accidents / get things right*.'

3 In 2001, a hospital in the US introduced a *five-point / ten-point* checklist for doctors.

4 When the same checklist was used in Michigan, infections went down by *about a half / around two-thirds*.

5 Some doctors didn't want to use Gawande's checklist because it was *too long / too difficult*.

6 Most doctors said they *would / wouldn't* want a surgeon to use the list.

2 Look at the title of the article and the photos. Read the article quickly. What do these words refer to?

well-known | eight | luxury | imagination

A famous list: Desert Island Discs

One evening in 1941, a man called Roy Plomley was sitting at home when he got an idea for a new radio programme. He wrote a letter to the BBC with his idea, and the BBC loved it. In 1942, they started to put the programme on the radio with Plomley as the presenter, and now, over seventy years later, the programme is still going strong on British radio. The name of the programme? Desert Island Discs (aka DID).

The idea of the programme is this: each week, someone well-known is invited to the programme – often an actor, a singer, a politician or someone from TV. In recent years, people like actor Colin Firth, adventurer Bear Grylls, celebrity cook Jamie Oliver and novelist J. K. Rowling have been guests. And what does the guest have to do? Well, he or she has to imagine that they have been cast away on a desert island, but that they are allowed to have eight pieces of music with them. The programme is an interview with the guest, talking about their life and work, and the eight pieces of music that the guest talks about are mixed in.

After some initial programmes, the list of eight songs was added to: guests are now also allowed to choose one book and one special, luxury item to have with them on the island. That certainly brought some cool ideas. The writer of children's books, Allan Ahlberg, asked for 'a wall to kick a football against', while famously pale-skinned singer Annie Lennox asked for suncream. And, perhaps not surprisingly, writer J. K. Rowling asked for 'an endless supply of pens and paper'.

From the very beginning, DID was incredibly popular, and it still is – there have been thousands of programmes. Plomley was the presenter for every episode until he died in 1971, and since then there have only been three other presenters. The programme's opening and closing music has never changed, and for British people it is immediately recognisable as the DID theme music.

There have been some memorable guests. One of the most controversial was an opera singer, Elizabeth Schwarzkopf, whose eight records included seven of herself singing – though, to be fair, it did seem that no one had explained the concept of the show to her well enough!

The idea of choosing just eight pieces of music to listen to forever, while you're completely alone in the world, is one that seems to capture people's imagination. What would you choose to have with you? Of course, if you like music at all, it's almost impossible to come up with a list of only eight pieces of music without leaving out things that you love. But that, perhaps, is part of the beauty of the whole DID concept.

3 Read the article again. Answer the questions.

1 How did Desert Island Discs start?

2 Who are the guests on the programme?

3 What ten things can guests take with them to the island?

4 How many presenters have there been?

5 What was different about the opera singer's choice of music?

6 What is the difficult part of making a list of eight pieces of music?

4 Imagine you could be a guest on DID. What eight pieces of music would you choose? And what would your book and your luxury item be? Write a short paragraph.

DEVELOPING WRITING

Advice for travelling – an email

1 Read the emails quickly and answer the questions.

1 What is the climate of Laura's holiday destination?

2 What five items of clothing does Sean suggest taking?

3 What four essential items does he suggest taking?

Hi Sean

I live in a nice warm place but soon I'm going to travel to northern Sweden in winter, so it's going to be really cold, maybe wet too. I'm looking forward to the trip but I'm really not very sure what I should take. Can you help?

Laura

Hi Laura

That's great that you're going somewhere very different from home! But you're right, it's important to think about what to take. OK, well the first thing of course is clothes.

- Take a hat and wear it, it's the best protection against the cold. Even better if it's one that covers your ears.

- Take sweaters and coats, but it's better to think about wearing several layers of thin clothing rather than single, heavy items.

- Take at least one good pair of waterproof shoes, otherwise your feet might get cold and/or wet and that's really not what you want!

- A pair of gloves is always a good idea too, as long as they're light and waterproof.

Then, there are other essential items. Think about taking these things:

- a pair of sunglasses if you're going to be anywhere where there's snow – the bright reflection off snow can hurt unprotected eyes.

- some sunscreen. In winter? Yes – the wind can burn your skin too, so protection is good.

- lip balm to stop your lips getting sore with wind and cold.

- some simple medicines to help with colds and runny noses – always useful, especially if you're going to be a long way from a town.

So, there you go, Laura. Hope this helps and have a great holiday!

Sean

2 Read Sean's email again. Answer these questions.

1 What's the best kind of hat to take?

2 What's better than a single, heavy sweater?

3 What should the shoes protect you from?

4 What should gloves be like?

5 Why should you take sunglasses in winter?

6 How can you protect your lips?

7 When is it especially useful to have medicines with you?

3 Answer these questions about the email.

1 How does Sean introduce his reply?

2 How does he separate out the different things he suggests taking?

3 Each thing comes with an explanation of why Laura should take it. How does Sean indicate reasons? (There are several different ways.)

4 You're going to write an email to a friend who wants advice about what to take on holiday. Read what the friend writes. Choose a, b or c for your answer.

Hi …
I'm going on holiday to **a)** a really hot place **b)** your town/city **c)** a place you know really well. But I'm not sure what to take with me. Can you give me a nice, simple list of ideas please?
Thanks!
Jim

5 Write your answer. Write 150–200 words.

CHECKLIST ✔

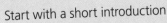

Start with a short introduction

Use bullet points for your list

Consider clothes and other things (essential items)

For each thing, give a reason for taking it

LISTENING

1 🔊 24 Listen to Alan, Beth and Colin talking. Complete the information.

Three things I couldn't live without

Colin	Beth	Alan
1 *phone*	1 _____	1 _____
2 _____	2 _____	2 _____
3 _____	3 _____	3 _____

2 🔊 24 Listen again. Mark the statements T (true), F (false) or DS (doesn't say).

1 Their friend Jacky has gone away for a weekend with her parents. ☐

2 Jacky isn't happy that she can't take her phone. ☐

3 Colin realises he doesn't need his MP3 player if he's got his phone. ☐

4 Beth's third choice is based on the fact that she likes the colour blue. ☐

5 Alan thinks it's sad if you can only think of three things you can't live without. ☐

6 Beth doesn't like serious discussions. ☐

7 Alan doesn't accept Colin's first idea for his third thing. ☐

8 Colin considers himself to be a good guitar player. ☐

3 Write your list of three things that you couldn't live without, and why.

1 _____

_____

2 _____

_____

3 _____

DIALOGUE

1 Put the dialogues into the correct order.

1

☐	ADAM	Like the way that guy last night did? I think if I was a contestant on that programme, I'd have shouted at him.
☐	ADAM	But do you think you would behave better? I mean, in a situation like that.
1	ADAM	Are you watching that reality show about people stuck on an island?
☐	ADAM	He certainly will. Well, unless one of the other people starts behaving even worse.
☐	BRIONY	Good question. And you know, I think I'd be OK, as long as the other people didn't make me angry.
☐	BRIONY	Yes, I think it's great. I love watching people behaving badly!
☐	BRIONY	And that's always a possibility, right? Listen, why don't we watch the next episode together?
☐	BRIONY	Me too. He was awful. If he carries on like that, he'll be voted off next week.

2

☐	ANGIE	Of course I will, don't worry. Why wouldn't I look after it?
☐	ANGIE	Not true. I looked after it. I just gave it back later than I'd promised.
1	ANGIE	Can I borrow your tablet?
☐	ANGIE	Of course I would have. But OK, don't lend me the tablet. I don't mind.
☐	BRENDAN	No, it's OK. You can borrow it. Otherwise you'll never talk to me again. Just joking, Angie!
☐	BRENDAN	Why? Well, I remember you didn't really look after the camera I lent you.
☐	BRENDAN	Well, yes, I suppose so – as long as you promise to look after it.
☐	BRENDAN	Right. And if I hadn't reminded you, you'd never have given it back.

2 Choose one of the two scenarios. Write a 6–8 line dialogue between the two people.

1 Elena wants Amy to go shopping with her. Amy remembers previous shopping experiences with Elena, that weren't very good. But in the end, Amy agrees.

2 Chris wants to go and see a concert. But Chris's parents will only let Chris go if a friend goes too. Sammy doesn't really like the music in the concert.

Speaking part 2

1 Look at this pair of photos. How do you think the people feel in each photo?

2 ◀◎25 You are going to listen to Alexander talking about the photo (you will also hear an examiner). Here are some things Alexander says. Which photo is each phrase about? Write A or B in the boxes. Then listen and check.

1 It doesn't look like they're enjoying it very much. ☐
2 Apparently they've been shopping. ☐
3 It looks as though they're enjoying the nice weather. ☐

4 I don't know exactly where it is but it could be Sweden or Denmark. ☐
5 I don't think they are really very happy. ☐
6 They seem to be having a good time. ☐

3 In each of the sentences 1–6 in Exercise 2, Alexander softens what he says. For example, he doesn't say 'They have been shopping' – he says 'Apparently they've been shopping.'

How does he soften his statements in the other five sentences?

Exam guide: individual 'long turn'

In Part 2 of the First speaking exam, there will be two examiners and two candidates in the room. You will be given two pairs of photos. You will be asked to talk about one of the pairs. You have to talk about them for about a minute. The examiner will tell you what to talk about concerning the two photos.

The examiner will say, for example:
X, I'd like you to look at your two photos and compare them.
Say what you think the people feel about being outside in these situations.

● You only have one minute so try to keep talking, stopping as little as possible.
● Try to use as wide a range of vocabulary as you can.
● Make sure that you do what you're asked to do – here, for example, don't describe the photos but talk about what you think the people are feeling and why.
● Speak clearly and as confidently as you can – confidence always helps!

---

4 ◀◎25 Listen again. How well did he do? Grade his performance.

Give him 1 star for 'could do better', 2 stars for 'good' and 3 stars for 'excellent'.

1 His voice is clear. ★ ★★ ★★★
2 His word and sentence stress are good. ★ ★★ ★★★
3 He talks fluently. ★ ★★ ★★★

4 He uses a good range of vocabulary. ★ ★★ ★★★
5 He sounds natural. ★ ★★ ★★★

5 Imagine you are an exam candidate yourself. Do the same task that Alexander did and ask a friend to listen to you and grade your performance.

CONSOLIDATION

LISTENING

1 🔊26 Listen to Dave and Maggie. Tick the things that Maggie is taking with her on holiday.

A ☐ B ☐ C ☐ D ☐ E ☐ F ☐

2 🔊26 Listen again. Answer the questions.

1 What negative things does Maggie talk about with regard to camping?

2 Why are tablets for stomach ache on her list?

3 Why does Dave agree that it's a good idea for Maggie to take medicines with her?

4 What condition did Maggie's parents state for her taking her tablet with her?

5 What does Dave say that makes Maggie panic?

6 What does Dave say about the next time they see each other?

GRAMMAR

3 Circle the correct options.

1 I'm going to have a shower as soon as I *get / will get* home.

2 If I spoke another language as well as you do, I'd *be / was* really pleased with myself.

3 If you *don't / won't* help me, I'll be really angry with you.

4 By the time you read this, I *will have arrived / will have been arriving* in the USA.

5 I can't see you tomorrow night – we *go / are going* to my uncle's birthday party.

6 If you'd told us where you were going, we *wouldn't be / wouldn't have been* so upset now.

7 This time tomorrow, we'll *watch / be watching* my sister's first appearance on TV.

8 By next year we *will live / will have lived* in this flat for more than ten years.

VOCABULARY

4 Match the sentence halves.

1 Our weekend was ruined when my mum came ☐
2 I've got a really good feeling ☐
3 She's decided she wants to carry ☐
4 Everything will be fine unless ☐
5 We weren't sure what to do, but Sue came ☐
6 We'd better go now, otherwise ☐
7 It isn't easy to work ☐
8 Let's just take a moment, please, and run ☐

a up with a brilliant idea.
b we get home really late.
c down with a really bad cold.
d about the game tonight.
e through the names again.
f out the research, no matter what.
g we'll be late getting home.
h out why that happened.

5 Complete the words.

1 Can I just p _ _ _ _ out that this isn't your first mistake.

2 We're all looking f _ _ _ _ _ _ _ to seeing you again.

3 I hate camping, so I'm really d _ _ _ _ _ _ _ _ this weekend!

4 I don't care what you do, p _ _ _ _ _ _ _ you don't get me into trouble.

5 It's not a big problem, so why are you getting so w _ _ _ _ _ _ up about it?

6 I'm not sure about our new house, but my parents feel quite p _ _ _ _ _ _ _ about moving there.

7 We got to the address on time, but it t _ _ _ _ out to be the wrong place.

8 I guess it'll be OK, but I have to say I'm a bit a _ _ _ _ _ _ _ _ _ _ about tomorrow's test.

DIALOGUE

6 Complete the dialogue with the phrases in the list. There are three you won't use.

so far | I'm afraid so | Anyway | for a start
cheer up | get my hopes up | go for it
Fair enough | I think so

PAUL   So what happened at your interview? Oh, you look pretty unhappy. Did it go badly?

ANNIE   ¹_____. In fact, almost everything went wrong. I was late ²_____.

PAUL   Oh dear. Were they angry about that?

ANNIE   ³_____. Well, they certainly didn't smile much. And the woman who was the main interviewer said they could only give me 15 minutes.

PAUL   ⁴_____, I suppose.

ANNIE   Yes, you're right. After all, they have other things to do. ⁵_____, they asked me some questions but I don't think I answered them especially well.

PAUL   Well, ⁶_____. If you don't get the job, you can try other places.

ANNIE   But there aren't any other places! Oh well, I'll just have to wait until they contact me, I suppose.

READING

7 Read the article and answer the questions.

Who …

0   was turned down by several record companies?
    The Beatles

1   once had a job driving trucks? _____

2   was an influence on other people in his field?
    _____

3   was famous for E.T. (among other things)? _____

4   was sometimes called by another name? _____

5   was turned down for a job by a famous film maker?
    _____

6   ended up with an art gallery showing his work? _____

7   has won Hollywood awards? _____

WRITING

8 Choose one of the people in the article. Write a dialogue of 8–10 lines between that person and a person who said 'No' to them.

Your dialogue can be either:
- at the time the person said 'No', OR
- after the rejected person became famous.

Being rejected

A lot of people who became incredibly successful had to get past a lot of rejection. Very famously, The Beatles went to several record companies before they finally found one that was willing to record one of their songs. (Imagine how the other companies felt a few years later!) But they weren't alone. Here's a short list of rejections.

Steven Spielberg, the wealthiest film director in Hollywood and a man who has won two Oscars for Best Director, tried three times as a young man to get into the University of Southern California School of Theater, Film and Television – and three times, they said 'No'. So he went somewhere else, but didn't like it much and dropped out. Thirty-five years later, and after establishing his hugely successful career, he went back and finished his degree. Imagine – if he hadn't dropped out, he wouldn't have made films like E.T.

Claude Monet is recognised now as one of the great Impressionist painters. But he was laughed at by the other painters in the Paris Salon, which was a kind of club for painters and writers who met to discuss their ideas and their work. They refused to let him join them. Little did they know that Monet would become a huge influence on other artists, and would become extremely famous in his own lifetime. There is also now a gallery in Paris called l'Orangerie that displays some of his most famous paintings and which is visited by thousands of people every year.

Charles Schultz – do you know that name? Maybe not, but you probably know the 'Peanuts' cartoons that he invented and drew for decades before he died in 2000, and which have been published in various languages all over the world. He started doing cartoons in high school, but the school wouldn't publish them in their annual end-of-year celebration book. Even Walt Disney turned him down for a job before he started his cartoon career.

In 1954, **Elvis Presley** played for just one night at a famous concert hall in Nashville. The manager fired him immediately afterwards and told him to 'go back to driving a truck'. Presley, of course, went on to become the most famous singer in the world for many years – his nickname was 'The King' and he sold millions of records and made several films too.

So, it takes persistence to make it, no matter how good you are! As our examples here show, even if you get turned down several times, you can still make it as long as you have determination and self-belief.

GRAMMAR

I wish and *If only* SB page 86

1 ★☆☆ **Read the sentences. Does the person regret their present situation or do they regret a past action? Write PA (past) or PR (present).**

1 If only I didn't have so much homework. ☐
2 I wish I had said what I felt. ☐
3 If only I'd gone to bed earlier. ☐
4 I wish I could speak French. ☐
5 If only I hadn't said anything. ☐
6 I wish John would call. ☐

2 ★★☆ **Complete the sentences with the correct form of the verbs in the list.**

let │ listen │ be │ work │ help
understand │ get │ not get

1 I wish my dad would _____ to me.

2 If only he _____ what it's like to be a teenager.

3 I wish he had _____ me go to the party.

4 I wish I hadn't _____ so angry with him.

5 If only I could _____ him.

6 I wish he _____ so angry.

7 If only I had _____ less strict when he was a child.

8 I wish I hadn't _____ so much when he was younger.

3 ★★☆ **Complete the sentences using the words in brackets in the correct form.**

1 I don't feel very well. _____ I _____ so much. (If only / not eat)
2 You have to be 18 to watch this film. _____ I _____ so young. (I wish / not be)
3 Debbie's so complicated. I _____ what she was thinking. (I wish / know)
4 I don't know how to do this homework. _____ I _____ attention in class today. (If only / pay)
5 I can't hear a thing today. I _____ to that concert last night. (I wish / not go)
6 I'm not good enough to get in the school team. _____ I _____ football better. (I wish / play)
7 I really wanted to see that film. _____ you _____ me the ending. (I wish / not tell)
8 We've still got one more hour of school. _____ we _____ home now. (If only / can go)

4 ★★★ **Read the sentences and write down two regrets for each one; one past and one present.**

0 I've got a really bad headache.
   I wish I could go home. If only I hadn't spent all night playing on the computer.

1 My sister plays her music really loud.
   _____

2 I haven't got any money.
   _____

3 We've got a Maths test today.
   _____

4 My computer's broken.

Pronunciation

Linking: instrusive /w/ and /j/
Go to page 120.

I would prefer to / it if, It's time,
I'd rather / sooner `SB page 89`

5 ★ ☆ ☆ **Circle the correct form.**

1 I would rather you *don't / didn't* ask so many questions. I'm tired.
2 I'd prefer *to invite / inviting* George than Henry.
3 It's time Natalie *starts / started* behaving more like an adult.
4 Would you prefer it if we *take / took* a break for five minutes?
5 I'd sooner *spend / spent* the money on a new TV.
6 I'd prefer it if they *don't / didn't* come this evening.
7 We'd sooner you *don't / didn't* let your dog come in our garden.
8 It's time someone *takes / took* this problem seriously.

6 ★★☆ **Complete the dialogue with the correct form of the verb in brackets.**

ANA   Dan. It's time we ¹_____ a talk. (have)
DAN   Really? Now? I'd prefer ²_____ TV. (watch)
ANA   That's the problem. You never want to talk.
DAN   OK, we can talk but can't it wait? I'd rather we ³_____ after this film. (talk)
ANA   And I'd sooner we ⁴_____ now. (chat)
DAN   OK. All right. What is it? Make it quick though, please.
ANA   OK. Can I have the remote?
DAN   The remote?
ANA   Yes, the remote control.
DAN   OK, here you are, but why do you want it?
ANA   Because I'd prefer we ⁵_____ the news. (watch)
DAN   Hey, I was watching that film!

7 ★★★ **Complete the second sentence so it has a similar meaning to the first sentence using the word given. Use between two and five words including the word given.**

1 Play tennis or volleyball? Tennis is my choice.
   PREFER
   I _____ tennis.
2 You need to learn to ride a bike.
   TIME
   It's _____ to ride a bike.
3 The film starts too late. I can't watch it.
   DIDN'T
   If _____ start so late.
4 I'd prefer to eat at home.
   WE
   I'd rather _____ at home.
5 I told Dad a lie. That was a mistake.
   WISH
   I _____ Dad a lie.
6 Can we go to France this year, rather than Italy?
   PREFER
   I _____ we went to France this year.
7 Someone needs to tell her.
   TOLD
   It's _____ her.

GET IT RIGHT! 👁

would rather / would prefer

Learners often use the wrong verb form after *would rather* or *would prefer*.

✓ *They **would rather say** …*
✗ *They would rather to say …*
✓ *I'd **prefer to go** on holiday.*
✗ *I'd prefer go on holiday.*

Complete the sentences with *would rather* or *would prefer*.

1 I _____ leave school and get a job than go to university.
2 Jo _____ to sleep on it and decide in the morning.
3 We _____ you weren't so unreasonable.
4 _____ (you) start your degree course now or have a gap year?
5 Olivia _____ to have a lie in tomorrow morning if that's OK.
6 Josh _____ play tennis than watch a film.

VOCABULARY

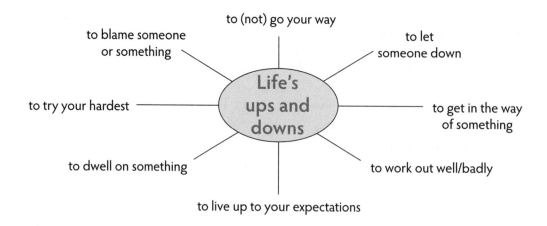

to (not) go your way

to blame someone or something

to let someone down

to try your hardest

Life's ups and downs

to get in the way of something

to dwell on something

to work out well/badly

to live up to your expectations

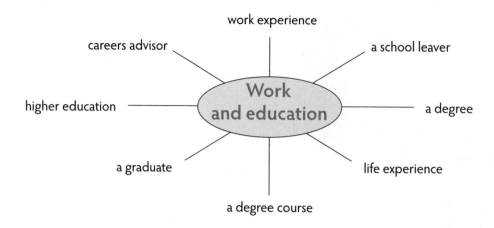

work experience

careers advisor

a school leaver

higher education

Work and education

a degree

a graduate

life experience

a degree course

Key words in context

instantly	Most people, when they see a photo of the Eiffel Tower, recognise it **instantly**.
lie in	Tomorrow is Sunday and I'm going to have a **lie in** until 11 am. Don't wake me!
overdramatising	It wasn't that bad. I think you're **overdramatising** things a little.
overreacting	It's only a small cut. I think calling an ambulance would be **overreacting** a little.
perfection	That meal was absolutely delicious. It couldn't have been better. It was **perfection**!
perspective	Try and see it from her **perspective**. Then maybe you'll understand why she did it.
simplistically	To put it very **simplistically**, global warming is a result of there being too many cars.
sleep on	I'm not sure. Can I **sleep on** it and let you know tomorrow?
snap	Mr Coyne's in a bad mood today. He **snapped** at me just because I asked him a question.
unreasonable	I only asked for an extra £10 pocket money a week. That's not **unreasonable**, is it?

Life's ups and downs SB page 86

1 ★★☆ **Complete with the words in the list.**

get | dwell | expectations | way
let | hardest | blame | work

five little rules of life

1 Always try your _____ –
it's the best that you can do.

2 Don't always _____
someone else when things don't
go your _____ .

3 Don't let the little things
_____ in the way of the
important stuff.

4 Don't _____ on things
too long when they don't
_____ out well.

5 If you feel that someone has
_____ you down ask
yourself, 'Do I always
live up to their _____
of me?'

2 ★★☆ **Which of the rules in Exercise 1 should these people follow?**

1 'The referee was terrible. He clearly wanted the other side to win and made all his decisions to ensure that they did.' ☐

2 'Why did I fail the test? Why? I should have studied harder. I shouldn't have gone out last weekend. I'm going to regret not taking it more seriously for the rest of my life.' ☐

3 'I can't believe I didn't win. I spent months preparing for this race. I don't know what else I could have done.' ☐

4 'I can't believe Jamie didn't come to my party. He promised he would. And it's not the first time. I just can't rely on him for anything.' ☐

5 'I can't get started on my revision until I've got my room tidied and answered all my emails.' ☐

Work and education SB page 87

3 ★☆☆ **Unscramble the letters to make eight words or expressions about work and education.**

1 greede _____
2 greede orusce _____
3 rescare voraisd _____
4 cohols reveal _____
5 orwk nepixeerec _____
6 file epierecexn _____
7 degrauat _____
8 hhiegr incadeuto _____

4 ★★☆ **Complete the sentences with the words and expressions from Exercise 3.**

1 I'm not going to go on to _____ .
2 My _____ is in journalism.
3 Get a Saturday job. It's good to try and get a bit of _____ while you're still at school.
4 There aren't so many good jobs for _____ these days because so many people are going to university.
5 More and more _____ are going to university these days.
6 I think _____ is more important than education.
7 His _____ lasts for four years.
8 I had no idea what I wanted to do after I left school so I went to see a _____ .

5 ★★★ **What do you plan on doing when you leave school? Write a short text (50 words) and use at least four of the phrases from Exercise 3.**

_____
_____
_____
_____
_____
_____
_____
_____
_____
_____
_____
_____
_____

READING

1 **REMEMBER AND CHECK** Look back at the quiz on page 88 of the Student's Book. Which questions could 1–6 be options for?

1 Can you make sure you put them back in the wardrobe afterwards? ☐

2 You spend all your time on that thing. ☐

3 There's no school today. ☐

4 OK, but we're going to have to run. ☐

5 I'm trying to concentrate. ☐

6 I'm going to have to try harder next time. ☐

2 Read the book review. Who are the 'villains' that the author introduces, and what should the reader do with them?

The Teen's Guide to World Domination:
Advice on Life, Liberty, and the Pursuit of Awesomeness by Josh Shipp

It's no secret that the teenage years can be tough. But despite the difficulties they are also potentially some of the most thrilling times of our lives. They are the times when we discover all the amazing things that we are capable of and start to make them happen. They are the beginning of our journey into life as an adult. As with other long and exciting journeys what we need is a guide to help us through it. *The Teen's Guide to World Domination: Advice on Life, Liberty, and the Pursuit of Awesomeness* is exactly that; a book for teenagers to help them achieve their very best. From cover to cover is it full of insightful advice that will inspire and entertain anyone who reads it.

The author Josh Shipp knows what he's talking about. He was a problem teenager himself but these days he makes his living helping teenagers help themselves and helping their parents understand them better. He is also a regular contributor on teen issues for many different media companies.

To help us through the teenage years, John introduces us to a colourful cast of villains which we must face and defeat before we can reach the 'awesomeness' that all teenagers are capable of. If we want to achieve our true potential, these are some of the obstacles that might try and get in our way:

Vampires – All those bad things in life that you find yourself attracted to even though you know they are bad. Stop them from trying to lead you the wrong way and learn how to stay far away from them.

Robots – The people in your life who want to control you. They want to see you do the same things they do. Break free from their programming and find your own path through life.

Ninjas – You think they are your friends but really they're just using you to get what they want. Don't be fooled by them. It's time to fight back.

Puppies – They seem cute and cuddly but are they really? Look closer. Don't be blinded by their immediate appeal. Beware of the danger they hold.

Pirates – The mean kids in life who make your life a misery. There's no room for them in your world. Find out how to keep them out of your life.

Ghosts – We all get it wrong from time to time and these are the memories of mistakes you have made that make it difficult for you to move forward. But you need to break free from the past. It's time to forget them and move on.

Zombies – The complainers who want to share their unhappiness with you. You don't have the time to listen to them. Stay clear of their negativity and don't let them bring you down.

3 Read the review again. Which one of Shipp's 'villains' are these people are talking about?

1 My dad wants me to be a doctor, just like him. _____

2 The last time I had to stand in front of the class and talk I made a fool of myself. I never want to do it again. _____

3 Jenny Wilson says that life is never fair. I always feel depressed when I hang out with her. _____

4 I've got a feeling that Bobby only likes coming over to my house because he likes my sister. _____

5 I waste far too much time on the Playstation. I wish I could stop playing it all the time. _____

6 Robbie Dawson is a bully. I'm scared to go to school because I know he's there waiting for me. _____

4 Choose one of the 'villains' and write a short text (60–80 words) to describe this person or thing.

DEVELOPING WRITING

An essay about teenage life

1 Read the essay. What three things would the writer like his school to offer?

> ## WHAT COULD SCHOOLS DO TO MAKE LIFE EASIER FOR TEENAGERS?
>
> The school I go to has a clear aim; to help its students achieve the best grades they can so that they can leave school with the qualifications they need for the next stage of their lives. I expect this is true of most schools around the country.
>
> While this is certainly a very useful intention, it doesn't really take into consideration that teenagers are more than just empty beings to fill with information. There are many more important issues that young adults need to address other than just learning the facts. We need help learning how to deal with conflict at school and at home. We need to be able to talk about how our emotions affect us. We need to be given information about what opportunities we will have when we leave school. Sadly our school offers very little help in these areas.
>
> Of course, I know it's asking a lot to expect schools to deal with all this on top of their academic responsibilities, but there are things they could do to help make a difference. First and foremost I'd like to see a dedicated welfare officer, someone on hand throughout the school day to talk students through any problems they might be facing. Secondly, I'd love it if our school had a careers office, a place where you could find out what life is really like in the working world. This would certainly be useful in helping us make more informed decisions when we leave. Finally, it would be good to see a mentoring scheme, a system in which each first-year student has a 'friend' in one of the top years to show them around. This would help make the transition from primary school to secondary school a lot smoother.
>
> I accept that a school's role is primarily to educate but I'm sure that it wouldn't take too much to implement these ideas and make our lives just a little bit easier.

2 At 320 words this essay is too long. Choose four sentences that could be cut to help shorten it.

3 Complete these sentences from the essay.

1 I'd like to see a dedicated welfare officer, _____ on hand throughout …

2 I'd love it if our school had a careers office, _____ where you could find out …

3 It would be good to see a mentoring scheme, _____ in which each first-year …

4 Read the essay again and complete the mind maps. Then add three more ideas of your own.

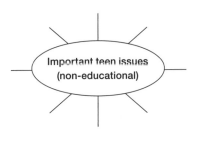

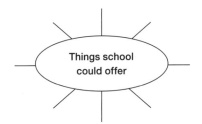

5 Write your answer to the question in around 200 words.

Write your own checklist.

87

LISTENING

1 🔊 28 **Listen to the conversations. Match the names Steve, Rob or Alan with the things they are complaining about.**

1 _____

2 _____

3 _____

2 🔊 28 **Listen again and answer the questions.**

1 What is Lucy using Steve's tablet for?

_____

2 Why isn't she using her own tablet?

_____

3 What did Lydia want to ask Rob?

_____

4 Why is Rob angry with Lydia?

_____

5 Why does Alan want Cindy to keep the music down?

_____

6 What does Cindy agree to bring him?

_____

3 🔊 28 **Put the words in order to make lines from the dialogue. Listen again and check.**

1 tablet / rather / without / you / I'd / take / my / asking / didn't

2 off / room / you / my / took / I'd / shoes / walked / before / your / into / you / sooner

3 too / it / door / shut / if / you / kept / I'd / prefer / your

DIALOGUE

1 **Put the lines in order to make the dialogue.**

☐ PAUL A meal – that's a really good idea. Chinese or Indian?

☐ PAUL Well, we've got to do something. How about going shopping?

☐ PAUL OK, Italian it is. Shall I invite Francis and Olivia?

1 PAUL So we've passed our exams. What are we going to do to celebrate?

☐ PAUL OK, no problem. So let's go to the cinema.

☐ RUBY I'd rather not. There's not really anything I want to buy.

☐ RUBY Neither. I'd prefer to try out that new Italian on Hope Street.

☐ RUBY That's a good question. I haven't really thought about it.

☐ RUBY No, I'd rather just go with you.

☐ RUBY I'd sooner go out for a meal.

2 **Complete these mini-dialogues with your own ideas.**

1 A Would you like to watch some TV?

B I'd prefer _____

2 A How about organising a party for the end of the school year?

B I'd sooner _____

3 A Let's take the bus to Gran's.

B I'd rather _____

3 **Choose one of these opening lines and write a short dialogue (8–10 lines). Use an example of _I'd prefer, I'd rather_ and _I'd sooner_.**

'What shall we do tonight?'
'What do you want to do this weekend?'
'Where do you want to go on holiday this summer?'

_____

_____

_____

_____

_____

_____

_____

_____

_____

_____

_____

Listening part 4

Exam guide: multiple-choice questions

In this part of the exam you hear an interview with someone or an exchange between two people. You hear each extract twice.

- On the exam paper there are seven multiple-choice questions each with three possible answers. You have to choose the correct answer.
- Before you listen, read through the questions and options to prepare yourself for the kind of things you will hear. Read the questions carefully so you know exactly what they are looking for.
- You will need to listen out for attitudes, opinions, purpose, feelings, main points and details.
- The wrong options will often contain similar information to what you hear. They will also often contain words and phrases from the listening. Be careful because this doesn't mean they are correct.
- Use your second listening to confirm answers you have already chosen and answer those questions you weren't able to the first time round.

1   🔊 29   **You will hear an interview with Abby Jones talking about her gap year before going to university. For questions 1–7 choose the best answer (A, B or C).**

1   Why didn't Abby go straight from school to university?
  A   Because she never thought her exams would be good enough to get her into university.
  B   Because she waited too long to make a decision.
  C   Because she changed her mind about what career she wanted to do.

2   Why was Abby a little frightened about taking a year off?
  A   She thought she'd lose contact with her friends.
  B   She felt she might not find employment when she finally finished university.
  C   She had no idea what to do with all that time.

3   Why didn't Abby want to spend her year off working for the police?
  A   Because as a volunteer she wouldn't get paid.
  B   Because it might put her off her dream job.
  C   Because she realised the year off was an opportunity to experience something new.

4   Why did Abby's dad mention Thailand to her?
  A   Because he had a relative out there.
  B   Because he thought she could get a job in a hotel there.
  C   Because he knew it was somewhere she'd always wanted to go.

5   What did Abby do with the money she earned?
  A   She used it to pay back her parents for the flight ticket.
  B   She gave some to her dad's cousin for letting her stay in her house.
  C   She saved it so she could go travelling.

6   What did Abby study in Thailand?
  A   how to cook Thai food
  B   how to speak Thai
  C   how to teach English

7   What advice does Abby offer school leavers?
  A   take a year off
  B   travel the world
  C   think carefully about what you want to do with your year off

GRAMMAR

Reported speech (review) SB page 94

1 ★☆☆ **Rewrite the sentences as reported speech.**

0 'Jamie is late,' said Jo.
Jo / said / that / Jamie / be / late
Jo said that Jamie was late.

1 'I like horror stories,' said Matt.
Matt / said / that / he / like / horror / stories
_____

2 'I will see you at the concert on Saturday,' said Ali.
Ali / said / that / he / see / us / at / the concert / on Saturday
_____

3 'I have been to Spain many times,' said Helen.
Helen / said / that / she / be / to / Spain / many times
_____

4 'I'm looking forward to seeing you,' said Elif.
Elif / said / that / she / look forward / to / seeing / me
_____

2 ★★☆ **Rewrite Jamie's text messages in reported speech.**

1 I'll see you all at Jake's birthday party on Saturday.

Jamie said that _____

2 It's half-time. Our team has scored two goals.

Jamie said that _____

3 I can't get tickets for the concert. It's sold out.

Jamie said that _____

4 We're not playing Sunnyhill School. They've cancelled the match.

Jamie said that _____

5 Our Maths teacher quit yesterday. I can't believe it.

Jamie said that _____

6 I haven't done enough revision for the History exam.

Jamie said that _____

3 ★★★ **Read the statements from an article about Twitter. Then report them.**

1 In 2013, it took one week for users to send a billion Tweets.

2 40% of registered Twitter users have never sent a Tweet.

3 Twitter is available in 25 languages now.

4 75% of world leaders use Twitter.

5 Barack Obama's victory Tweet was the most retweeted Tweet in 2013.

6 The country with the most Twitter users in 2014 was China.

7 Twitter has become the fastest way to break news.

8 Twitter will become more like Facebook in the future.

The article said:

1 _____
2 _____
3 _____
4 _____
5 _____
6 _____
7 _____
8 _____

4 ★★★ **Report five messages you tweeted or texted this week.**

1 _____
2 _____
3 _____
4 _____
5 _____

Reported questions and requests

SB page 95

5 ★★☆ **Report the questions. Use + *if*, + *to* or + question word.**

0 'Do you want to be a journalist when you leave school?'

I asked her if she wanted to be a journalist when she left school.

1 'Why do you want to be a journalist?'
My friend asked me _____

2 'Think of a name for the school online magazine.'
My teacher asked me _____

3 'Interview a foreign correspondent for the school magazine.'
The editor of the school magazine asked me

_____

4 'Prepare some questions for the interview.'
She asked me _____

5 'Which countries have you reported from?'
I asked the foreign correspondent, Jeremy Hope,

_____

6 'Have you reported from any war zones?'
I asked him _____

7 'Can you get me a glass of water?'
She asked me _____

Verb patterns SB page 97

6 ★★☆ **Match the sentence halves.**

1 The journalist apologised ☐
2 The police officer warned the driver ☐
3 The driver regretted ☐
4 The journalist agreed ☐
5 The public criticised the newspaper ☐
6 The director of the company accused the journalist ☐
7 The man denied ☐
8 The newspaper admitted ☐

a leaving his vehicle.
b to interview the witness.
c of upsetting his staff.
d robbing the bank.
e for upsetting the girl.
f not to leave his vehicle.
g to printing incorrect facts.
h for printing incorrect facts.

7 ★★☆ **Circle the correct form.**

1 Daisy regretted *for telling* / *telling* her story to the newspaper.
2 The pop star accused the newspaper *of printing* / *printing* lies about him.
3 The media criticised the politician *for failing* / *to fail* to explain his actions.
4 The film star apologised *for being* / *of being* late for the interview.
5 The victim's wife agreed *speaking* / *to speak* to the press.
6 The boy admitted to *drive* / *driving* the car without a licence.
7 The bank manager admitted *to make* / *that he had made* a mistake.
8 The boy was warned *about entering* / *for entering* the empty building.

8 ★★★ **Now write true sentences for you.**

1 I regret _____
2 I apologised _____
3 I admit _____
4 My mum/dad/friend warned me _____
_____
5 I agreed _____

GET IT RIGHT!

say and *tell* in reported speech

Learners often make mistakes with *say* and *tell*.

✓ I **told Ian** about the news.

✗ I ~~said to Ian~~ about the news.

✓ He **said that** he was amazed.

✗ He ~~told that~~ he was amazed.

Tick the sentences that can use both *say* and *tell*. Rewrite them using the other verb. Add any other words if necessary. Put a cross if the sentence can't use both.

0 We didn't tell Jess anything about the party. ✓
We didn't say anything about the party to Jess.

1 I don't think politicians ever tell the truth. ☐
_____

2 The teacher told John that his essay was amazing. ☐
_____

3 Charlotte said she felt the same way. ☐
_____

4 You need to say something to them to keep them quiet. ☐
_____

5 Please tell her to keep in touch. ☐
_____

VOCABULARY

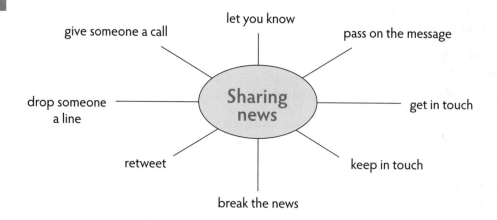

Reporting verbs

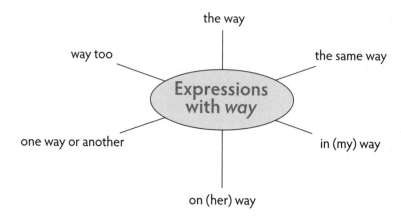

Key words in context

bias	Many newspapers have a **bias** towards one political party or another. They give that party their support.
correspondent	My brother is a sports **correspondent** for a local newspaper. He reports on all sporting events in our local area.
distress	The journalist's questions had caused the boy a lot of **distress**. He was very upset after the interview.
efficiently	The machine is very slow at the moment. We need it to work more **efficiently**.
epidemic	The number of children in the area with measles has increased. There is now a measles **epidemic**.
impact	The mobile phone has had a huge **impact** on the way people communicate.
impartial	The witness was not **impartial**. She was the victim's sister.
newsworthy	That story is definitely **newsworthy**. It should be reported in the news.
prejudice	Different social groups and even groups from different generations often show **prejudice** towards each other. They don't try to understand each other.
resign	The manager **resigned** after the scandal. He has left his job.

Sharing news [SB page 94]

1 ★☆☆ **Match the sentence halves.**

1 I'll let ☐
2 He broke ☐
3 I'll drop ☐
4 Give me ☐
5 I'll pass ☐
6 He got ☐

a you a line.
b on the message.
c in touch with me last week.
d you know.
e a call.
f the news gently.

2 ★★☆ **Complete the mini-dialogues with the phrases in the list.**

got in touch | let you know | retweeted
drop you a line | pass on the message
give me a call | keep in touch
break the news gently

1 A I can't believe you're moving to Australia. That's the other side of the world.
   B Don't worry, I'll _____. We can Skype often.

2 A I can't tell Jane about the puppy. She'll be really upset.
   B I'll tell her. And don't worry. I'll _____.

3 A Mike's arriving next week, have you _____ with him yet to find out where he's staying?
   B No, not yet, I'll email him this evening.

4 A Wow! Your followers have _____ your comment about the book 200 times. Is that a record for you?
   B I think so.

5 A I've just got a message about football practice. It's been cancelled on Sunday.
   B Thanks, I'll _____ to the rest of the team.

6 A What time's the rehearsal on Wednesday?
   B I'm not sure. When I find out, I'll _____.

7 A Right, I'm off then. I'll see you at school tomorrow.
   B Yes, _____ when you get home. And don't forget we've got an English test tomorrow.

8 A Well, this is goodbye then. I hope you like the new school.
   B I'll miss this place and all of you, of course. When I've settled in, I'll _____.

Pronunciation

Linking: omission of the /h/ sound
Go to page 120. 🔊

Reporting verbs [SB page 97]

3 ★★☆ **Complete the sentences with a reporting verb that means the same as the words in brackets.**

1 The actor _____ the newspaper of misquoting him. (claim)

2 The editor _____ to everybody that he had made a mistake. (tell)

3 The photographers _____ for upsetting the actor. (say sorry)

4 The judge _____ the photographers to stop following the pop star. (tell)

5 The sister of the Manchester United footballer _____ selling her story to a newspaper. (be sorry for)

6 The editor was angry. He _____ her for printing the story. (complain about)

7 The council _____ to approve the building plans. (say they will)

8 The council had _____ the local residents that the building was unsafe. The boys ignored the 'Danger! Keep Out' sign on the gate. (notify)

WordWise [SB page 99]

4 ★★☆ **Complete the mini-dialogues with the expressions in the list.**

the way | the same way | in my way
on her way | one way or another | way too

1 A I'm glad you've agreed to be a volunteer at the Cat's Protection Society.
   B Yes, so am I. It's great to be with people who feel _____ I do about cats.

2 A Have you finished that report for the school newspaper yet?
   B Not yet. I'll get it done by 5 pm, _____.

3 A Did you take that online test?
   B Yes, I think the questions were _____ easy.

4 A I love _____ Instagram lets you see what all your friends are up to.
   B Yes, so do I.

5 A Have you seen this message from Sarah?
   B Yeah, I wanted to ask her about that.
   A You'll be able to ask her in person. She's _____ here now.

6 A Hey, Mark. Move over a bit. You're _____. I'm trying to watch a film.
   B Sorry, I didn't realise.

READING

1 REMEMBER AND CHECK Answer the questions. Then check your answers in the article on page 93 in the Student's Book.

1 Who is Jack Dorsey?

2 What has Twitter had the biggest impact on?

3 How many characters can you have in a Tweet?

4 What has Twitter made it easier for young people to do?

5 What can people organise on Twitter?

6 What has Twitter given ordinary people?

2 Read the article. What went wrong in each of the three examples?

WHAT NOT TO DO ON SOCIAL MEDIA – A CAUTIONARY TALE

One simple Tweet or one wrong photo on Facebook can get you into trouble with the law, stop you from getting a job and even lose you your job. Something that takes us seconds to do can have huge consequences. Here are some examples of where things went wrong for these three social media users.

The Facebook invite

In 2012, in the little town of Haren in Holland, a girl was celebrating her sixteenth birthday. She decided to have a party and invite her friends to her house. She created an invitation on Facebook but she didn't make it private. She sent it to friends who sent it to their friends and it spread across the Internet. Her party invitation was passed on, not to one hundred people, not to one thousand people but to thirty thousand people. The party was cancelled but three thousand people still turned up. Riot police were sent to the town to keep the party-goers away from the house and the girl had to leave her home. The party turned into a riot. Rioters set fire to a car and damaged street signs and lamp posts. Six people at the party were injured and twenty people were arrested.

A bad tip

Ashley Johnson, a 22-year-old waitress from North Carolina in America, was unhappy with a tip she received from two customers dining at the restaurant where she worked. The two customers had sat at their table for three hours and Ashley had stayed at work an hour longer, waiting for them to finish their meal. Consequently, she wasn't happy when they only gave her a tip of $5. Unfortunately she vented her anger on Facebook. She called them 'cheap' and mentioned the name of the restaurant where she worked. Insulting customers or speaking disapprovingly of them on social media was against company policy. Ashley Johnson was fired.

Flying out of a job

Not one, but thirteen crew members were sacked by a famous airline for their messages on Facebook about the airline. They criticised customers, which again was against company policy. They also discussed private company business on the website. They said that the planes were infested with cockroaches and that the airline had replaced the jet engines of some of the planes four times in one year. These comments should have been made privately to the company. They should not have been discussed on social media. Subsequently they were all sacked.

According to the Internet security company, Proofnet, eight per cent of employers in the USA have fired employees after viewing their postings on social media sites. Seventeen per cent of employers have issued warnings to their staff after finding postings that went against company rules and policies. We all need to be more careful about what we post on social media. Remember a Tweet is there forever and you can never be completely sure who will view the photos on your Facebook page. So always think before you post that 'fun' photo or tweet that 'careless' thought. Think what consequences it might have in the future.

3 Read the article again and complete the reported sentences with between two and four words.

The article said that …

1 a girl's party invitation posted on Facebook had been passed on to _____ people.

2 the party _____ a riot.

3 Ashley Johnson was _____ she had received from two customers.

4 Ashley had had to stay at work _____ waiting for the customers.

5 thirteen crew from an airline had been sacked for _____ about the airline.

6 the messages said that the airline _____ jet engines of some planes.

7 17% of employers _____ to their staff about postings on social media.

8 we all need _____ about what we post on social media.

4 Write a short paragraph giving advice on how to use social media responsibly.

DEVELOPING WRITING

An article for the school magazine

1 Read Kate's article 'Around the World with Twitter' and find the answers to these questions.

1 Who? ....

2 When? ....

3 Where? ....

4 What? ....

5 How? ....

Around the world with Twitter

[1]......................

This is the amazing story of how one man travelled the world using Twitter.

[2]......................

In March 2009, Paul Smith, a British blogger, writer and former radio executive from Gateshead in the Northeast of England travelled around the world using the social media network Twitter. His journey started with an overnight ferry from Newcastle to Amsterdam and ended in New Zealand on the other side of the world.

[3]......................

Paul had the idea whilst he was in a supermarket. Two days later, he wrote his first Tweet and 'Twitchhiker' was born. Paul's aim was to travel as far from his home as possible in thirty days without spending any money on accommodation or travel. The only money he could spend was on food and drink and things that he could fit in his suitcase. The other rules were that he could only make travel plans three days in advance. If he was stuck anywhere for more than 48 hours, he had to go home.

[4]......................

After thirty days and with the aid of over 11,000 Twitter followers, Paul Smith had travelled as far as Stewart Island in New Zealand, and he had also raised over £5,000 for charity. Twitter had made it possible for one man to travel round the world, relying only on the kindness of strangers. What other great adventures can Twitter make possible? So far no one else has attempted the challenge. Maybe you or I could be next. Or maybe we'll look for a new challenge.

---

2 Read these tips for planning your article and number them in the correct order. Then label Kate's article.

☐ **Closing paragraph and a quotation**
Find something that sums the article up in a few words. You can also end your story with a link to more information on the Internet.

☐ **Lead sentence**
Grab your reader's attention.

☐ **Main body**
In this paragraph, answer 'How' and 'Where' and go into more detail. What happens? What are the events of the story?

☐ **Introduction**
Tell your readers 'Who?' 'What?' and 'When?'

3 You are going to write an article. Choose one of the topics below. Use the Internet to help you research your article.

1 an interesting way to travel round the world

2 an interesting train journey

3 a recent news story that caught your attention

Complete the plan below for your article.

Lead sentence

Introduction

Main body

Closing paragraph

4 Now write your article. Write between 200–250 words.

Write your own checklist.

CHECKLIST ✓

LISTENING

1 🔊 31 **Read the sentences below. Then listen and tick the correct statement.**

The news story for the school magazine will be about …

a   the civil war in Sierra Leone. ☐

b   an orphan from Sierra Leone who became a star ballerina. ☐

c   a woman who opened an orphanage in Sierra Leone. ☐

2 🔊 31 **Listen again. Mark the sentences T (true) or F (false).**

1   Marcus says that he doesn't want to have a story about ballet in the school magazine. ☐

2   Sarah agrees with Marcus that ballet isn't a good subject for the school magazine. ☐

3   Tom says that he likes ballet. ☐

4   Tom tells Marcus that Michaela DePrince's father had been killed in a civil war in Sierra Leone. ☐

5   After Michaela had been adopted by an American couple, she attended a ballet school. ☐

6   Michaela says that she will open a school and teach art with the money she earns from her book. ☐

DIALOGUE

1 **Complete the dialogue with the phrases in the list.**

Have you heard | have you heard about
did you know | guess what | You'll never believe

JAMIE   ¹_____? Somebody stole Leo's bike yesterday.

MARIE   No way! That's awful. It was a new bike as well. He got it for his birthday. I must tell Cathy. Here she comes now! Cathy, ²_____ Leo's bike?

CATHY   Yes, his bike was stolen. But, ³_____.

MARIE   What?

CATHY   The thief has brought the bike back. He left it at the school gates this morning, and he left a note on the bike. ⁴_____ what it said.

JAMIE   Come on then. Tell us.

CATHY   It said, 'Thanks for lending me the bike. My son didn't like it so I've brought it back.' Can you believe it?

MARIE   You're joking! Well at least Leo got his bike back.

JAMIE   Yes, that's good news. But ⁵_____ that five bikes were stolen from the school grounds last year? And none of them were brought back. Leo's lucky.

PHRASES FOR FLUENCY

SB page 99

1 **Match the sentence halves.**

1   It will cost us £10, ☐

2   It's OK. <u>Don't</u> ☐

3   Karen, where ☐

4   I need some fresh air. Let's go for a walk ☐

5   <u>In any</u> ☐

6   Stop asking me. <u>It's none of</u> ☐

a   <u>on earth</u> have you been?

b   <u>your business</u>.

c   <u>or something</u>.

d   <u>at least</u>.

e   <u>bother</u> sending me a reply.

f   <u>case</u>, you know it's dangerous.

2 **Complete the dialogues with the underlined phrases from Exercise 1.**

1

LUCIA   Would you like to write an article about Twitter for the school magazine?

TANYA   It sounds interesting. I'd like to do it. But do you need me to write it right away? I'm really busy now. I don't know how _____ I'd fit it in.

LUCIA   No, it's OK. You can write it next week. We won't print the magazine until the end of the month. _____, you're the best person to write it.

2

TIM   Did Jeremy tell you what happened?

LUKE   No, he didn't. I asked him but he said _____.

3

MATT   Let's ask Nick to come to the park with us _____.

CHRIS   Good idea. We can take our bikes.

4

NAOMI   My mum said that Claude Monet had painted over 1,000 paintings and there would be _____ 500 paintings on display at the exhibition.

EMILY   Well, it sounds like you're going to be very busy looking at paintings so _____ sending me any texts or emails or anything. You can tell me all about it when you get back.

Writing part 2

1 Read the task.

You have seen an announcement in the school magazine.

> **Book Reviews Wanted**
>
> Write a review of a book you have recently read. Your review should include the title and author's name, a brief description of the characters, the plot and themes of the book. Would you recommend this book to others? Give your opinion of the book. The best reviews will be published in the next edition of the magazine.

Write your review.

2 Read the model answer and underline ten mistakes. Then write the correct word.

The Everest Files **by Matt Dickinson**

The Everest Files is action adventure thriller for young adult readers. Its the first book in a series of three books and it was inspired by Matt Dickinson's own climb up Mount Everest.

Ryan, an eighteen-year-old American, is on a gap year adventure. He is working for a medical charity in the Nepal. A local girl asks him to find out why her sixteen-year-old Sherpa friend Kami never have come back from an expedition up Mount Everest with a wealthy American politician. Some says he's alive and others say he's dead. Ryan, who is determined and adventurous, can't resist the challenge. Kami's story takes place at the magnificent and terrifying slopes of Mount Everest and it is very moving. The story is fast paced and there are some very tense moments.

One of the themes of the book is how climbers disturb the natural order of the Nepalese mountains and Mount Everest itself is one of the main characters of this dramatic mystery. Another theme of the book is the importance of showing respect for other cultures, and the author is dedicated his book to the three Sherpas who he climbed up Everest with.

The Everest Files is very much exciting and the ending was unexpected. I really enjoyed to read it and I recommend it to both girls and boys who like learn about other cultures and love adventure. I'm looking forward to the second book in the series.

3 Circle the adjectives in the table that the writer uses in his/her book review. Then add some adjectives to the table.

	positive	negative
Main character	kind-hearted, determined, adventurous, _____	rude, wicked, _____
Characters	funny, friendly, brave, _____	evil, unfriendly, cruel, _____
Plot	amazing, excellent, exciting, clear, _____	terrible, awful, confusing, _____
Story	brilliant, fast-paced, moving, _____	boring, upsetting, _____
Setting	magnificent, _____	terrifying, _____
Ending	amazing, unexpected, _____	ridiculous, disappointing, _____

Exam guide: writing a review

In this part of the exam you are asked to write a text from a choice of text types. Here, we practise how to write a book review.

- Remember to include some adjectives to make your review interesting.
- Include some relevant vocabulary for a review, for example: *characters, plot, setting, themes,* etc.
- Your description of the plot needs to be clear and concise and you must be careful not to give the ending away.
- You need to choose a book that you have strong opinions about. Your opinion can be negative or positive.
- Explain who you would recommend the book to.

4 Now write your review. Write 140–190 words.

CONSOLIDATION

LISTENING

1 🔊 **32** **Listen to news on a local radio programme. Tick the three things that are talked about.**

  a Someone who is looking for a job. ☐

  b Someone who has left their job. ☐

  c Someone who might lose their job. ☐

  d Someone who appeared in a magazine. ☐

  e Someone who has won a prize. ☐

2 🔊 **32** **Listen again. Complete the missing information in each sentence with no more than five words.**

  1 Mr Godber said he _____ about the time he worked for the club.

  2 Mr Godber thinks some things _____ way.

  3 Mr Godber wants to _____ his future.

  4 Ms Green has _____ for sending the Tweet.

  5 The college director thinks the Tweet had _____ of the college.

  6 It's possible that the college _____ Ms Green's contract.

  7 Annabel Lee won her prize by _____.

  8 Annabel will be going _____ a week.

GRAMMAR

3 **Circle the correct options.**

  1 My brother asked me *to help / would I help* him.

  2 I wish it *isn't / wasn't* raining.

  3 I think it's time we *get / got* in touch with them again.

  4 I asked him *if he wanted / did he want* to read the book.

  5 If only you *told / had told* me yesterday, then I could have done something about it.

  6 I'm sure he wishes now that he *didn't buy / hadn't bought* that cheap tablet.

  7 He asked me why *had I left / I had left* the cinema in the middle of the film.

  8 I really would prefer it if you *didn't / don't* put olives on the pizza.

  9 Take any flavour you want, but I'd sooner you *leave / left* the vanilla one for me.

VOCABULARY

4 **Match the sentence halves.**

  1 He apologised ☐

  2 I've always regretted ☐

  3 They're on holiday but they dropped ☐

  4 My parents warned me ☐

  5 Try not to dwell ☐

  6 He's been accused ☐

  7 You promised to do it but you really let ☐

  8 As soon as I find out, I'll let ☐

  9 I wanted to go, but other things got ☐

 10 My attempts to be nice to him didn't work ☐

  a on things that happened in the past.

  b me down.

  c for being late.

  d you know.

  e me a line yesterday.

  f not learning to play a musical instrument.

  g not to make too much noise.

  h of taking money that wasn't his.

  i in my way.

  j out very well.

5 **Complete the words.**

  1 It was really a matter of luck – things just didn't go my w ___.

  2 I didn't do it! I d ___ ___ ___ it completely!

  3 Well it wasn't her fault so you can't b ___ ___ ___ ___ her for what happened.

  4 She lives in Canada now, so we keep in t ___ ___ ___ by email and social media.

  5 She's finished university – she got her d ___ ___ ___ ___ ___ last month.

  6 It doesn't matter that you didn't win – at least you tried your h ___ ___ ___ ___.

  7 I'm going to the factory twice a week to get some work e ___ ___ ___ ___ ___ ___ ___.

  8 The concert was OK, but it didn't really live up to my e ___ ___ ___ ___ ___ ___ ___ ___ ___.

  9 It's bad news and I don't know how to b ___ ___ ___ ___ it to him.

 10 She's very well qualified – she's a g ___ ___ ___ ___ ___ ___ of a top university.

DIALOGUE

6 Complete the dialogue with the words or phrases in the list. There are two extra ones.

at least | don't bother | I'd rather | on earth | in any case
none of her business | I'd prefer it | never guess

MAX You'll ¹_____ what I heard.

DI What?

MAX Jack South had a huge argument with his parents and they've grounded him. He isn't allowed to go out with his friends for ²_____ two weeks!

DI Well, Max, ³_____ you didn't tell me things like that. I'm not very interested. And ⁴_____, it might not be true.

MAX Well, I wasn't sure it was true, until Sue Jones told me, and she's never wrong about these things.

DI Well, it's ⁵_____. Nor yours, either, to be honest.

MAX Well I'm sorry, I didn't think you'd be so upset. It's just a bit of news, that's all.

DI Sorry, Max, but it's gossip. If you hear more gossip like that, please ⁶_____ telling me, OK?

MAX OK, Di. Well, it was nice to see you anyway – I think.

7 Read the article and answer the questions.

1 How is meditation believed to have started?

_____

2 When did it start to become adopted and practised in the West?

_____

3 How is meditation usually done?

_____

4 To do walking meditation, how do you need to walk?

_____

5 What do you need to concentrate on while walking?

_____

6 Where is the best place to do walking meditation?

_____

7 When should you not do walking meditation?

_____

8 What are the benefits of practising?

_____

WRITING

8 Write a paragraph of about 120 words about the way(s) that you relax best.

Ways to relax – Number 12 in our series
Walking meditation

A lot of people around the world practise meditation – a technique for becoming very calm and relaxed. It's most commonly practised by essentially concentrating on only one thing and cutting out the outside world. There isn't a lot of recorded history about meditation, but we know that it started a long, long time ago. It's believed that meditation may have been discovered as long ago as the days of primitive people who hunted for wild animals, and then, when cooking the meat over fires, began to stare at the flames and think in a different, more relaxed way. And there are Indian writings called 'tantras' which mention meditation, and these tantras are around 5,000 years old.

Thousands of years after meditation took off in the East, it began to be adopted in Western cultures too, becoming popular mostly around the middle of the 20th Century. Researchers also began looking at the effects of meditation, and more and more was understood about the many benefits it brought to its practitioners.

Now, most people think of meditation as something you normally do sitting down in a cross-legged position and with your eyes closed, and very often it is. But there is another kind of meditation that has recently been made popular by the Vietnamese teacher Thich Nhat Hanh: walking meditation.

People who do walking meditation say that it helps them get into a meditative state quite easily, through concentrating on the actual act of walking. You need to walk fairly slowly and calmly, of course, but not too differently from a normal pace. And as you walk, the idea is to get your mind to think about nothing else than what you and your body are doing: walking. Each time you find you're starting to think about something else, you try to bring your mind back, to concentrate on your feet and their contact with the ground, and how your arms swing as you walk.

It can be done anywhere, even in confined spaces – but most people say it is best practised outside, in an environment with nature around, if possible. You should do it for about twenty minutes and not combine it with anything else – don't do walking meditation while you're going to school, work or the shops. Do it as an activity for its own sake, it's much better that way. And don't think about your destination – walking meditation is all about going, not arriving.

Sounds easy? In a way it is, although like anything else, it needs practice and the more you do it, the better you get at it and the richer the rewards. It is a way towards dealing with the stresses and strains of everyday life, and towards living more peacefully. And, as Thich Nhat Hanh says: 'Peace is every step'.

GRAMMAR

Speculating (past, present and future)

SB page 104

1 ★☆☆ Do these sentences refer to the past, present or future? Write PA (past), PR (present) or F (future).

1 You might have left your passport at the hotel. ☐

2 Don't touch that frog. It may be poisonous. ☐

3 United are bound to lose. ☐

4 It could be Kevin who sent you the flowers. ☐

5 Her teachers say she's likely to pass. ☐

6 She can't have left the country. She hasn't got a passport. ☐

2 ★★☆ Circle the correct option.

1 The cat might *take / have taken* it.

2 Wow. That must *be / have been* exciting.

3 He can't *go / have gone* far. He's not wearing any boots.

4 The people at the information office must *know / have known* a good hotel.

5 Take lots of water. You're *bound to / could* get thirsty.

6 Come on. The man on the radio said the roads *are likely to / must* get really busy today.

3 ★★★ Use between two and five words to complete the second sentence of each pair, so that it means the same as the first sentence. You must also include the word in capital letters. Do not change the form of this word.

1 There'll be rain for sure this weekend. We're planning a picnic.
BOUND TO
_____ this weekend. We're planning a picnic.

2 They're speaking Portuguese so there's a chance they're Brazilian.
COULD
They _____ Brazilian because they're speaking Portuguese.

3 Toby got top marks in the test. I'm sure he spent all week studying for it.
MUST
Toby _____ studying to get top marks in the test.

4 Police believe there's a possibility one of the robbers worked at the bank in the past.
MIGHT
Police believe one of the robbers _____ at the bank in the past.

5 I don't think anyone will beat Federer at Wimbledon this year.
CERTAIN
I think _____ at Wimbledon this year.

6 The cat must be outside. I can't find it.
CAN'T BE
The cat _____. I can't find it.

7 Scientists think the population of our planet will probably pass 8 billion by 2030.
LIKELY
Scientists think the population of our planet _____ 8 billion by 2030.

Pronunciation

Stress on modal verbs for speculation
Go to page 121.

Cause and effect linkers `SB page 107`

4 ★☆☆ **Match the sentences or sentence halves.**

1 The football match was cancelled ☐
2 As a result of her hard work ☐
3 His parents took away his computer ☐
4 She's not very popular. ☐
5 Due to the high price ☐
6 She got a record contract ☐
7 Because of his high temperature ☐
8 He's quite short for his age. ☐

a because of his bad school report.
b Consequently not many people came to her party.
c as a result of her popularity on YouTube.
d his mother didn't let him go to school.
e due to crowd trouble.
f Consequently lots of people think he's younger than he is.
g not many children went on the school skiing trip.
h she raised £1,000 for charity.

5 ★★☆ **Complete the second sentence so it means the same as the first in each pair.**

I'm sorry I was late to school today, Sir…

1 My alarm clock was broken. I overslept.
As a result of _____
_____ .

2 My room's a mess. I couldn't find my tie.
Due to _____
_____ .

3 My bike's got a flat tyre. I couldn't ride it to school.
Because of _____
_____ .

4 I've got a twisted ankle. I couldn't run to the bus stop.
_____ as a result of
_____ .

5 There was an accident. The bus journey was really slow.
_____ due to
_____ .

6 I arrived at 9.30. The school gate was locked.
I couldn't get into school because of

6 ★★★ **Think of three different ways to finish each of these sentences.**

1 The launch of the rocket was delayed
due to _____
because of _____
as a result of _____

2 Alan didn't get to be an astronaut
due to _____
because of _____
as a result of _____

3 The astronaut had to return early from the space station
due to _____
because of _____
as a result of _____

4 The school trip to the space centre was cancelled
due to _____
because of _____
as a result of _____

GET IT RIGHT!
Modals of speculation

Learners often make mistakes when using modals of speculation, either using the wrong modal or the wrong tense.

✓ You **can't** have been very happy when you heard the news!
✗ You ~~mustn't~~ have been very happy when you heard the news!
✓ You should **have helped** her to finish her project. She didn't finish it on time.
✗ You should ~~help~~ her to finish her project. She didn't finish it on time.

Choose the correct option.

1 A Samantha got top marks in her exams!
B She *must / may* be over the moon.
2 Dave's been to London once before. He *might / must* know a good restaurant.
3 You *can't / mustn't* be serious! I'm not doing that.
4 I might *have seen / see* the film but it's not really the genre I usually go and watch.
5 The film was thrilling. No one could have *made / make* it better than him.
6 We *must / might* be very early. There's no one else here!

VOCABULARY

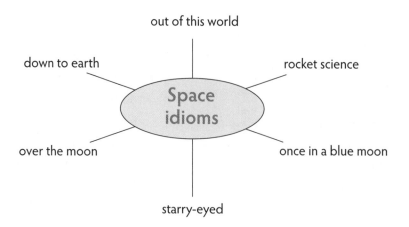

Space idioms: out of this world, down to earth, rocket science, over the moon, once in a blue moon, starry-eyed

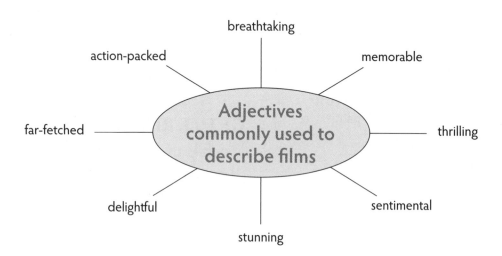

Adjectives commonly used to describe films: breathtaking, action-packed, memorable, far-fetched, thrilling, delightful, sentimental, stunning

Key words in context

abducted	Some people believe they have been **abducted** by aliens and taken to their spaceships.
beyond	Don't go **beyond** that line. It's dangerous.
destruction	The **destruction** of the rain forests must stop.
drifting	All they found of the plane was part of the wing **drifting** in the Atlantic Ocean.
eclipse	There's a lunar **eclipse** tonight when the Earth's shadow completely covers the moon.
galaxies	**Galaxies** are made of billions and billions of stars.
greed	Mankind's **greed** for money will cause the destruction of our planet.
interrupted	I don't like being **interrupted** when I'm speaking.
invaded	Our town's been **invaded** by flies this summer. No one knows where they've come from.
mankind	**Mankind** is the most intelligent species on the planet but it doesn't always act that way.
mission	The spacecraft is on a **mission** to take photos of Jupiter.
oxygen	We need **oxygen** to breathe.
pretend	Let's start again and **pretend** that never happened.
reminder	The school sent a **reminder** that it would be closed on the 15th.
signals	This machine sends **signals** into the sky to try and contact alien life forms.
weapons	The police found several **weapons** in his house including knives and guns.
wreck	They showed photos of the train **wreck** on TV. It was a terrible crash.

Space idioms SB page 105

1 ★ ☆ ☆ **Match the sentences.**

1 His costume was out of this world. ☐
2 Come on, kids. It's not exactly rocket science. ☐
3 His fans are very starry-eyed. ☐
4 He's very down to earth really. ☐
5 They're over the moon. ☐
6 We eat out once in a blue moon. ☐

a They love absolutely everything he does.
b They've just got married and they're really happy.
c We hardly ever do it.
d It was really amazing.
e He's very normal and unpretentious.
f Anyone can make it.

2 ★★ ☆ **Match the pictures with the sentences in Exercise 1.**

A ☐

B ☐

C ☐

D ☐

E ☐

F ☐

Adjectives commonly used to describe films SB page 107

3 ★ ☆ ☆ **Find eight adjectives commonly used to describe films in the word search.**

G	D	E	L	I	G	H	T	F	U	L	E	A
N	S	P	Q	O	W	I	E	U	R	Y	J	C
I	Y	T	A	L	S	K	D	J	F	H	G	T
K	Z	M	U	X	N	C	B	V	R	G	R	I
A	L	A	T	N	E	M	I	T	N	E	S	O
T	Q	Z	A	W	N	X	S	I	E	C	R	N
H	V	F	T	B	G	I	L	Y	N	H	U	P
T	M	J	I	K	L	L	N	I	O	P	T	A
A	L	A	B	Y	I	K	S	G	E	I	S	C
E	L	B	A	R	O	M	E	M	A	E	L	K
R	U	E	H	A	C	R	A	C	S	O	G	E
B	U	T	F	A	R	F	E	T	C	H	E	D

4 ★★ ☆ **Circle the option which is NOT possible.**

1 The view from the top of the mountain was absolutely …
   a stunning   b far-fetched   c breathtaking

2 That was a really … meal – one that I won't forget for a long time.
   a thrilling   b memorable   c delightful

3 It was a really … game of football – the best I've seen for ages.
   a action-packed   b thrilling   c sentimental

4 The play was a bit … but I still enjoyed it.
   a sentimental   b delightful   c far-fetched

5 That high-speed car chase in the film was absolutely …!
   a action-packed   b thrilling   c delightful

6 They looked … on their wedding day.
   a memorable   b stunning   c breathtaking

5 **Think of a film (or a scene from a film) that is …**

1 stunning _____
2 a bit far-fetched _____
3 breath-taking _____
4 thrilling _____
5 too sentimental _____
6 action-packed from beginning to end
_____
7 memorable _____
8 delightful _____

READING

1 REMEMBER AND CHECK Answer the questions. Then check your answers in the article on page 103 of the Student's Book.

1 What do some people point to as evidence of alien activity on Earth?

2 Why is Hawkins so convinced there must be life 'out there'?

3 What kind of life does he expect it to be?

4 How does he suggest alien visitors might treat our planet?

5 What analogy does he make with the Native Americans?

6 What does Lord Rees suggest alien life forms might be like?

2 Read the blog. Which film does the writer consider to be the best alien film?

Top four films – Aliens

After the success of last week's post on space films, I thought I'd keep with the night sky this week for inspiration. So here they are, hand-picked for you, four of the very best alien films.

1 E.T. (1982)

A young and unknown Drew Barrymore and friends find a little alien hiding in the shed and spend the rest of the film trying to get him home, in Steven Spielberg's highly enjoyable (if a little sentimental) family film. With his huge eyes and glowing finger, E.T.'s cuteness won him millions of fans and showed us that not all aliens are trying to take over the world. An absolute classic that everyone should have seen by the age of 15. And who can ever forget the bike flying across the moon with E.T. in the basket – one of the most famous images in film history.

2 War of the Worlds (2005)

In 1898 H.G. Wells wrote one of the greatest science fiction novels of all time: War of the Worlds. In 1938 Orson Welles' radio production of it had people believing that aliens had really landed on Earth. In 1953 the first film version was released and became a huge success. Despite this, not many critics were all that excited when in 2005 it was announced that a Tom Cruise version was being released. However, they soon realised they were wrong and this modern version is one of the best sci-fi films of the last 20 years. Of course the special effects are great but it is Cruise's battle to save his family from the evil aliens that makes this film so exciting.

3 Men in Black (1997)

Unknown to most people, aliens are living on Earth disguised as humans. This is due to a secret government organisation which keeps an eye on the alien population. Will Smith and Tommy Lee Jones are special agents for this organisation. Their job is to make sure that the aliens behave and that the secret doesn't get out but neither of these things is always so easy to control. Great dialogue and special effects make this an entertaining science fiction comedy. And the success of the first film has already resulted in two sequels, both fun but not as good as the original.

4 District 9 (2009)

Saving the best until last, the most modern film on the list is also the least well-known, which is a shame since it's fantastic. Because of problems on their home planet, aliens arrive on Earth in need of help. The government agrees they can stay but places them in special areas. But the aliens soon get tired of being treated like second-class citizens and decide to fight back. Forget famous faces and a huge budget, this intelligent 2009 film from South Africa was as action-packed as any Hollywood blockbuster. It proves that not all films have to come from America. Of all the films on my list, this is the one most likely to make you think about the world we live in. I can't recommend it enough.

3 Read the blog again and mark the sentences T (true) or F (false).

1 Drew Barrymore wasn't famous when she starred in E.T. ☐

2 E.T. features a friendly alien. ☐

3 Critics were surprised by the 2005 version of War of the Worlds. ☐

4 Tom Cruise was in the first film version of War of the Worlds. ☐

5 Tommy Lee Jones and Will Smith play aliens in Men in Black. ☐

6 Men in Black II is the most enjoyable film in the series. ☐

7 The aliens in District 9 originally came to Earth peacefully. ☐

8 District 9 was filmed in Hollywood. ☐

4 Write a paragraph about your favourite film of all time.

DEVELOPING WRITING

A film review

1 **Read the review. Who are these characters?**

1 The Boov _____

2 The Gorg _____

3 Oh _____

4 Tip _____

Home (2015)

The latest alien blockbuster to hit our screens is the Dreamworks animated feature *Home* featuring the vocal talents of *Big Bang Theory*'s Jim Parsons (aka Sheldon), singer Rihanna and comedian Steve Martin.

When the Boov race of aliens from outer space come across Planet Earth they think they've found the perfect home. Having relocated all humans to big settlements in Australia, the Boov set about making the planet their own, safe from the attention of their enemies the Gorg. That is until one of them, the delightful but unfortunate Oh, accidentally sends out a house-warming party invitation, including the location, across the universe. It won't be long until the Gorg are with them, making Oh the most unpopular Boov on the planet. Can Oh, with the help of Tip, the last free human on Earth, save the planet?

Although clearly aimed at the younger end of the market, *Home* has plenty in it to appeal to parents and older brothers and sisters, making it an enjoyable 90 minutes for all the family. The story, while not the most memorable, is good enough to keep you watching and there are plenty of hilarious moments. Parsons and Rihanna will help the film's teenage appeal, while Martin will keep the parents happy. The perfect film for a rainy day this holiday.

Writing tip

In a review you will be asked to describe and give your opinion of something you have experienced. This can be a film or a play, or a book you have read. It might also be something like a restaurant, a holiday or a website.

- The aim of the review is to give the reader a clear idea of your experience so you will need to give a good description and explanation of the event.
- Use the first paragraph of your review to give some background details of the event.
- The second paragraph should contain a brief summary of the 'action'. In the case of a film, book or play this will be the story. Be careful not to give too much of the story away.
- The third paragraph should be more critical. This is where you say what you liked or didn't like.
- Finally, finish off your review with a recommendation.

2 **Look back at the review and answer the questions:**

1 What background information does the writer give in the first paragraph?

_____

2 Write a summary of the story in two sentences.

_____

_____

3 What did the writer like (or not like) about the film?

_____

4 What recommendation does the writer make?

_____

3 **Write a review of a film, book or play in around 200 words.**

Write your own checklist.

CHECKLIST ✔

☐ _____

☐ _____

☐ _____

☐ _____

LISTENING

1 🔊 34 **Listen to the three conversations. Label the people in the pictures, T (Tim), D (Dan) or J (Josh).**

 A

 B

 C

2 🔊 34 **Listen again and answer the questions.**

CONVERSATION 1

1 Who's going to play Romeo in the school play?
_____

2 How did Tim take the news that he wasn't Romeo?
_____

CONVERSATION 2

3 Why did Liz agree Dan could be in the band?
_____

4 What did Liz do when she heard Dan play?
_____

CONVERSATION 3

5 Why does Amelia think that Josh didn't get into the team?
_____

6 What are Josh's future sporting plans?
_____

3 🔊 34 **Compete the lines from the conversations. Listen again and check.**

1	HANNAH	He just walked out and said he didn't want to be in the play.
	SARA	O_____ d_____
2	LIZ	I had to ask him to leave, there and then.
	LIAM	H_____ t_____
3	CARL	The coach didn't want him apparently.
	AMELIA	W_____ a s_____
4	CARL	He didn't even make the second team.
	AMELIA	P_____ h_____

DIALOGUE

1 **Complete the dialogue with the missing lines. There are two extra lines.**

1 What a shame, but I'm sure he will give you another chance.

2 Oh dear. Better luck next time.

3 Poor you. Were you late?

4 Oh no. So you missed both break times?

5 How terrible. Why don't you try again?

6 Oh dear. So what's happened?

7 How terrible. That doesn't seem very fair.

JIM   What's up, Tina?

TINA   Nothing really. I'm just having a really bad day.

JIM   ☐

TINA   Well, first of all I missed the school bus so I had to walk to school.

JIM   ☐

TINA   Of course I was. So Miss Stevens wasn't very happy and her mood didn't get any better when I told her I'd left my homework at home. It was a Geography project that I'd spent days on. She said I'm going to lose five marks just because it's late.

JIM   ☐

TINA   That's what I told her and that's when she decided that I was being rude and that's why I had to spend break and lunchtime in the classroom on my own.

JIM   ☐

TINA   Yes, which was really bad because Mr Wilson was holding auditions for the school orchestra at lunchtime and I couldn't go.

JIM   ☐

TINA   I hope so, but knowing my luck today he won't.

2 **Choose one of these first lines and use it to write a short dialogue (8–10 lines).**

1 My dad says I can't go to Rob's party on Saturday.

2 I lost my wallet when I was shopping yesterday.

3 Have you heard? Sally's broken her leg.

_____
_____
_____
_____
_____
_____
_____
_____
_____

Speaking part 3

Exam guide: a two-way conversation

In part 3 of the speaking exam, you will be with one or two other candidates. Remember there is an interlocutor, who talks to you and manages the examination, and an examiner who only listens and assesses your English.

The interlocutor will ask you to look at some information which will include a question. For example: *Imagine your school is planning to start a new after-school club. Here are some ideas for the kind of club they could start and a question to discuss. First you have some time to look at the task.*

They will give you a short time to look at the task and then ask you to discuss the question together for about two minutes.

After this the interlocutor will ask you to come to a decision based on your first discussion. You will have another minute to do this.

Remember:

- Make sure you read the task carefully and answer the question that is written down. If you feel your partner is starting to talk about other things, try and bring them back to the topic.
- This is a joint task. It is important that you listen as well as talk. The examiner will want to see how well you can keep a conversation going. You can only do this by listening to what the other candidate is saying and responding to them appropriately.
- The examiner will also be looking for how well you can express your opinions and how you can back them up.
- For the second part, the interlocutor will ask you another question. This is not written down so if you don't understand, ask them to repeat it.
- In the second part you need to make a joint decision. The examiner will be looking to see how well you can argue your case, agree and disagree, negotiate, speculate, suggest and finally reach a decision.

1 🔊35 **Read through the exam question in the mind map and listen to two candidates discuss it. Answer the questions.**

Part 1

1 Make notes on what they say about each activity.

_____

Part 2

2 What question does the interlocutor ask them?

_____

3 What is their final decision? _____

2 🔊35 **Listen again. How well did they do in part 1? Grade their performance. Circle 1 star for 'could do better', 2 stars for 'good' and 3 stars for 'excellent'.**

	Candidate A (boy)	Candidate B (girl)
Answer the question	★ ★★ ★★★	★ ★★ ★★★
Listen to their partner	★ ★★ ★★★	★ ★★ ★★★
Express their opinions	★ ★★ ★★★	★ ★★ ★★★

3 🔊35 **Now listen to part 2 again and grade their performance.**

	Candidate A (boy)	Candidate B (girl)
Argue their case	★ ★★ ★★★	★ ★★ ★★★
Negotiate	★ ★★ ★★★	★ ★★ ★★★
Reach their decision	★ ★★ ★★★	★ ★★ ★★★

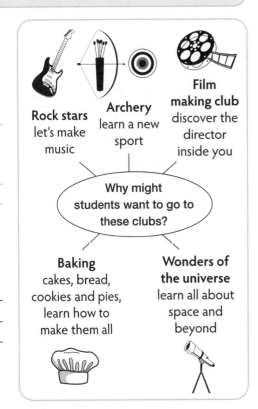

Rock stars let's make music

Archery learn a new sport

Film making club discover the director inside you

Why might students want to go to these clubs?

Baking cakes, bread, cookies and pies, learn how to make them all

Wonders of the universe learn all about space and beyond

4 **Work in groups of three. Two of you discuss the question while the other listens and gives feedback. Then swap roles.**

GRAMMAR

Passive report structures `SB page 112`

1 ★★☆ Complete the sentences with a passive report structure of the words in brackets. Then match the sentences to the pictures.

1 Roald Amundsen _____ to have been the first man to reach the South Pole. (know)

2 The climbers _____ to be halfway up the mountain. (believe)

3 The space probe _____ to arrive on Mars in six years' time. (expect)

4 The last dodo on Earth _____ to have died in 1662. (say)

5 The jug in the museum _____ to be more than a thousand years old. (think)

6 The last mammoths _____ to have lived on an island near Siberia. (know)

 A

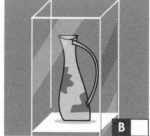 B

 C

 D

 E

 F

2 ★★☆ Complete the dialogue between a journalist (J) and a police inspector (I) using a word from column A and then a phrase from column B.

A

is │ are │ is │ was │ are

B

to have │ to have used │ to be │ to have suffered │ to be

J This evening there was a robbery at a jewellery store in the High Street. We're talking to Inspector Gordon about it. Inspector, do you already have a suspect?

I We do. The principal suspect is George Atkinson, a man who [1]_____ said [2]_____ connections with criminals in the east end of the city.

J And did he act alone?

I No. It appears there were two accomplices in the crime – they [3]_____ thought [4]_____ Atkinson's brother and brother-in-law. They are all dangerous men who [5]_____ known [6]_____ guns in the past.

J The theft involved an injury to someone in the shop, is that correct?

I Unfortunately, yes. A few hours ago, the manager of the shop [7]_____ thought [8]_____ in a critical condition, but an examination has been done and now he [9]_____ known [10]_____ only minor concussion.

J That's good news indeed. Thank you, Inspector, and good luck with your enquiries. Back to the studio.

3 ★★★ Write sentences using a passive report structure. Make them true for you.

0 London *is said to be one of the most expensive cities in the world.*

1 My home town _____

2 My house / flat _____

3 The most beautiful place in my country _____

4 The oldest building in my town _____

5 My favourite actor / actress _____

The passive: verbs with two objects

SB page 115

4 ★☆☆ **Read these sentences. Circle the direct object and underline the indirect object.**

0 They gave <u>the child</u> ⟨some medicine.⟩
1 The newsagent showed Penny the new magazine.
2 They offered the students free books.
3 Someone promised a room with a view to Kenneth.
4 The police didn't give any information to the reporters.
5 Someone sent me a strange email.
6 The bank manager offered her a job.
7 They sold faulty goods to their customers.
8 The company gave excellent conditions to their employees.

5 ★★☆ **Rewrite the sentences using the passive. Use the person as the subject.**

0 Someone offered me a cup of coffee.
   I was offered a cup of coffee.

1 Someone showed the photos to Jim.

2 They promised Jackie a part in the new play.

3 People ask film stars a lot of questions.

4 Someone gave Michael a horrible tie for his birthday.

5 People are going to pay the inventor a lot of money for her idea.

6 Someone sent an advertisement for sports equipment to my grandmother.

7 They offered my school a new IT centre.

8 No one told him the truth.

9 They didn't give the customers a refund.

10 The company didn't offer good benefits to the employees.

6 ★★★ **Write two complete sentences from each prompt. Put the more appropriate one first.**

0 Famous painting / give / art gallery
   The art gallery was given a famous painting.
   A famous painting was given to the art gallery.

1 The new students / tell / the class rules

2 My father / offer / a job in London

3 The new film / show / a large audience

4 A trophy / present / the winner

5 Alice / send / some flowers / for her birthday

GET IT RIGHT!
Passive

When using the passive learners often use the wrong tense. They also sometimes use the infinitive instead of the past participle.

✓ *We're all happy now that a decision **has been taken**.*
✗ *We're all happy now that a decision is taken.*
✓ *This picture had been **taken** 3 years before.*
✗ *This picture had been take 3 years before.*

All of the sentences contain an error. Rewrite them correctly.

1 There are still many places on Earth that haven't been explore yet.

2 A research trip to the glacier is taken this week.

3 He left the room after a joke has been made about him.

4 Every effort has made to find the missing man but to no avail.

5 A lot of progress is been made recently in Sam's work.

6 It's essential for good communication to be establish between nations.

VOCABULARY

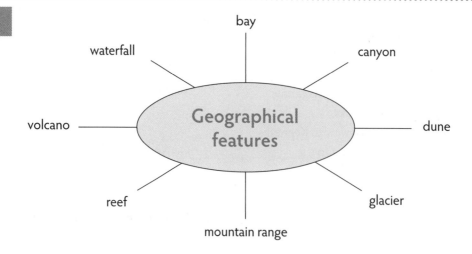

Verb + noun collocations

do	give	make	play	take
research	advice	amends	the fool	advantage of
	an example	a complaint	a joke	advice
	a speech	a deal	a part	a decision
		a decision		a joke
		an effort		a journey
		friends		a photo
		fun of		revenge
		a joke		
		a journey		
		a wish		
		money		
		progress		
		a speech		

Key words in context

advances	Medicine is improving all the time – the **advances** are fantastic.
conducted	They wanted to understand it better so they **conducted** lots of experiments.
determine	The police are working hard to **determine** exactly what happened last night.
endangered	There may soon be none of these animals left – they're **endangered**.
establish	If we want to work well with them, we need to **establish** good communication.
harsh	The terrible cold was made worse by the **harsh** wind that blew into our faces.
hold	It's a measuring jug – it **holds** exactly one litre.
motto	'Work hard and play hard' – that's my **motto**.
origins	Many words in English have Latin or French **origins**.
protection	You need to wear really warm clothes as **protection** against the cold.
species	Gorillas are just one of the many **species** that might become extinct before long.
territory	Many animals fight to defend their **territory** from outsiders.
tragic	They're destroying the forest to build a new road. I think it's **tragic**.
unsuitable	This film is **unsuitable** for children under the age of fourteen.

Geographical features SB page 112

1 ★★★ **Complete the crossword.**

1 Some sand ... in the Sahara Desert occasionally have snow on them.

2 The Grand ... in Arizona, USA was carved out of the rock by the Colorado river over many thousands of years.

3 In 2010 a ... in Iceland erupted and caused a lot of problems for planes.

4 There are three very high ... at Niagara on the border between Canada and the USA.

5 & 7 The Himalayas are a ... in Asia.

6 About 1,000 people live in floating villages in Ha Long ..., in Vietnam.

8 Visitors to Antarctica can see the Lambert .... It's the biggest ice formation in the world.

9 There are over 1,500 different species of fish in the Great Barrier ... in Australia.

Verb + noun collocations SB page 115

2 ★★★ **Circle the correct option.**

1 It's cruel to *make* / *take* fun of other people.

2 Dad *made* / *gave* a deal with the neighbour to share the path.

3 My little brother loves *playing* / *doing* the fool. It can be irritating sometimes.

4 Robert is very shy and finds it hard to *take* / *make* friends.

5 I've already *made* / *done* a lot of research for my project, but it isn't finished yet.

6 Lia was *taking* / *making* photos when she stepped back and slipped into the river!

7 The teacher told Jack's mother that he had *made* / *done* good progress that month.

8 I'd understand more easily if you *made* / *gave* me more examples.

3 ★★★ **Complete the sentences with verbs in the correct form.**

1 What would you _____ a complaint about in a restaurant?

2 What examples of bravery can you _____ ?

3 What is the longest journey you have ever _____ ?

4 What advice would you _____ to a friend who has just failed an exam?

5 If you had to _____ a speech in public, how would you feel?

6 What's the best joke you have ever _____ on someone?

4 ★★★ **Give your answers to the questions in Exercise 3.**

1 _____

2 _____

3 _____

4 _____

5 _____

6 _____

5 ★★★ **Rewrite the sentences using the words in brackets. Use the collocations in the Wordlist to help you.**

0 Do you hope for something on your birthday? (WISH)

   Do you make a wish on your birthday?

1 I think that I am getting better at the piano. (PROGRESS)

   _____

2 Sally tried hard to reach the top shelf. (EFFORT)

   _____

3 She said that she wasn't happy about the food (COMPLAINT)

   _____

4 Matthew accepted Kelly's offer of a lift home. (ADVANTAGE)

   _____

5 I forgot Jo's birthday, so to compensate, I took her out for dinner. (AMENDS)

   _____

READING

1 REMEMBER AND CHECK Match the places with the statements. There are two extra boxes. Then check your answers in the article on page 111 of the Student's Book.

A Caves ☐ ☐

B The Mariana Trench ☐ ☐

C The Amazon rainforest ☐ ☐

D Greenland ☐ ☐

E Deserts ☐ ☐

1 Drilling here has helped us to get a record of the Earth's environment.
2 Many of them are in China.
3 Many people are known to have died on expeditions here.
4 New species of insects and plants have been found here.
5 One example (Voronya) is in Georgia.
6 Only 2% has been explored.
7 People who live here live mostly near the coast.
8 We know more about the solar system than this place.

2 Look at the photographs and the title of the blog. Tick what you think the blog is about. Then read and check your ideas.

1 Someone hid some money in an old building. ☐
2 Someone paid a lot of money for an old house. ☐
3 Someone found money in an old house. ☐
4 Someone found treasure while building a house. ☐

Hidden treasure

When we hear the word 'exploration', we tend to think of people going off into deserted parts of the world, places like caves or deserts or ice-fields. But for a lot of people, exploration means finding out more about the town or city where they live: urban exploration (or UE). And the idea is that, instead of exploring the natural world, people start to explore man-made structures in cities, especially those places that city-dwellers usually don't get to see.

What kinds of places? Well, all kinds of places but often tunnels underground, old ruined buildings, or any kind of abandoned structure. Curiosity takes the explorers there and often, they record them by taking photos. Many urban explorers make a point of posting their photos on social media sites, and a lot of the photos are fantastic and attract a following.

It's also the case, of course, that unexpected things can happen. One example is from 2014 in Ontario, Canada. An urban explorer and photographer called Dave heard about a derelict house, and decided to go in to take photos, since this is what he loves doing. He moved around the house, taking photos of the rooms and the possessions that had been left behind. Then something caught his eye. In the corner of a bed, under an old mattress, something was sticking out. When Dave investigated, it turned out to be a bag, and inside the bag was about $7,000 in old American and Canadian bank notes. Some of the bundles of money had handwritten notes with dates from the 60s and 70s on them.

One of the principles of urban exploration is: 'take nothing but pictures, leave nothing but footprints'. So Dave had some more exploring to do – to try to find the owner of the money. He did some research into the house and who had owned it, and ended up making a phone call. The woman who answered the phone turned out to be the granddaughter of the last people to have lived in the house. Her grandparents had owned a fruit stall in Ontario, and kept their money under a mattress – and somehow, it had been forgotten. Dave gave the money to the woman, who was so grateful she cried.

Urban exploration can be a dangerous business – going into ruined buildings, or old tunnels, brings risks, and there have been instances of explorers being killed by, for example, falling off a roof or being hit by an underground train. It is also sometimes illegal – urban explorers, in their search for places where people never go and where they can take photos from angles that no one else has done, often end up going into places where they are not allowed to go. UE can uncover hidden treasure and bring joy, but it's important also to note that it can get explorers into a lot of trouble, both through physical risks and through the law.

3 Read the blog again. Answer the questions.

1 What examples are given of places that urban explorers go to?
2 Why did Dave go into the house?
3 How did he happen to find the bag?
4 Why did Dave decide not to keep the money?
5 How did he manage to find the granddaughter?
6 Where had the money come from?
7 Why did the granddaughter cry?
8 What are the two problems with urban exploration that the blog mentions?

DEVELOPING WRITING

A biography

1 Look at the photographs. What kind of person do you think the woman is? Write four or five words to say what you think.

adventurous , _____

_____

2 Read the biography of Ann Bancroft. Answer the questions.

1 What does she say her family were like?

_____

2 What were her first jobs?

_____

3 Name three of her achievements.

_____

4 What is special about most of her expeditions?

_____

5 What did her 2015 expedition aim to do?

_____

3 Label the paragraphs with the information.

1 Something special about her expeditions
2 Conclusion / summary of main point of interest about her
3 Introduction to the person / background
4 Main achievements

4 You are going to write a short biography of someone who explores things or places. It can be a real person (famous, or someone you know) or a fictional character from a book or TV show.

● Do some research about him/her, or if you don't know then make guesses.
● What kind of explorer is this person? Someone who actually goes to new places? Or someone who explored (for example) ideas, or history?

5 Write your biography. Write 200–250 words.

Write your own checklist.

CHECKLIST ✔

☐ _____

_____

☐ _____

_____

☐ _____

Ann Bancroft

[A] ☐ Ann Bancroft is an American writer and explorer. She was born in Minnesota and grew up in what she called a family of risk-takers. She became a PE teacher and then a wilderness instructor.

[B] ☐ In 1986 she got the chance to join an expedition to the North Pole, so she gave up her teaching job and went. After 56 days she became the first woman to get to the North Pole, walking and using a dog-sled. Later she became the first woman ever to get to both the North Pole and the South Pole, crossing the polar ice-caps to do so. Then she was the first woman to ski across Greenland.

[C] ☐ Bancroft often does expeditions with all-women teams – for example, in 1993 she took a group of women on skis to the South Pole. In 2001, she skied across Antarctica with Liv Arnesen.

[D] ☐ However, she doesn't only go to cold places. In 2015 she took a group – all women, of course – to India, walking along the river Ganges from the Himalaya mountains to the Bay of Bengal, in order to bring attention to the world's water problems. People could follow the expedition online. It was another example of Bancroft's desire to use her expeditions to educate people about the environment.

LISTENING

1 🔊 36 Listen to Mike giving a presentation to his class at school. The title of his talk is: 'Should we be doing more to explore space?' Tick the two reasons Mike gives in support of space exploration.

a We might find gases and minerals that aren't on Earth and that could help us. ☐

b We could develop places in space for people to live. ☐

c We might find intelligent life that could help us with our problems. ☐

d We could build stations in space to grow food for people on Earth. ☐

2 🔊 36 Listen again and answer the questions.

1 What does Mike think is one of the biggest problems on Earth?

_____

2 What does he think would be the consequence of not doing anything about it?

_____

3 Why does Steve disagree with Mike?

_____

4 What does Hazel say is 'never going to happen'?

_____

5 What does Angie say about money?

_____

6 What does Mike say might have influenced his ideas too much?

_____

7 How does the class generally react to Mike's talk?

_____

3 Write a short paragraph to say what you think about Mike's ideas.

Pronunciation
Linking: intrusive /r/
Go to page 121. 🔊

DIALOGUE

1 Put the dialogues in the correct order.

1

☐ ARNIE Well, perhaps you should be a little more open-minded. I tell you what – I'd like to see it again, so why don't you come with me? I'll pay.

[1] ARNIE We went to see that new film last night. It was really good.

☐ ARNIE Yes, OK, but a film's more than just one actor, isn't it? Maybe you didn't like those films for other reasons.

☐ ARNIE Really? Just because you don't like one of the actors?

☐ EMMA Yes, really. I've seen lots of films with him in and I didn't like any of them.

☐ EMMA The one with Mark Wahlberg? I don't like him. I don't want to see it.

☐ EMMA OK, you've persuaded me. But if I don't like it, I'll leave in the middle.

☐ EMMA Well, maybe – I mean, you could be right. But I'm still not going to see it.

2

☐ GRACE Oh but you should consider it, Billy. All you've got to do is read a book every two weeks. That's not much, is it?

☐ GRACE Have you heard about the new club at school? The book club?

☐ GRACE You know, I heard about an app for slow readers – you put it on your phone and it helps you start to read faster. Maybe that would help you. What do you think?

☐ GRACE Absolutely. You know I love reading, and I love talking! Are you going to join?

☐ BILLY Yeah, I heard about it. Have you joined it?

☐ BILLY Now that sounds like a great idea. I'll go and look for it now. And then maybe I'll join the club!

☐ BILLY Well, maybe not for you, but I'm a slow reader – a book a fortnight, that's a lot for me.

☐ BILLY No, no way. It's really not the kind of thing I'm into, you know.

2 Choose one of these two scenarios. Write a 6–8 line dialogue between the two people.

1 There's a school trip to an old city. Julie thinks she doesn't really want to go because she doesn't like old things. Jason tries to persuade her to go because it'll be interesting and there are some great places to eat in the city (etc.).

2 Paul is thinking of leaving school next year to get any job he can. He hasn't been doing well at school or in his exams. Sara tries to persuade him to stay another year and get some qualifications, which will help him get a better job when he leaves.

Speaking part 4

Exam guide: a discussion

(Before you do this page, make sure you have done the Exam page in Unit 11).

When you and your partner have finished part 3, you will start the last section of the exam. Here, the interlocutor will ask you to discuss topics related to what you talked about in part 3 with your partner. He/She will ask you some questions and leave you and your partner to say what you think. There are about four minutes for this final section.

In this section, it's important to remember to:

- give your opinion:
  I think … / The way I see it, … / In my opinion, … / My own view is that …
- say if you agree / disagree with your partner:
  Agree: *Yes, that's right. / Yes, I think X is right. / Absolutely! / I couldn't agree more.*
  Disagree: *Well, I'm not sure that I agree. / No, I don't really think so. / I'd have to say that I disagree. / No, I think X is wrong. / Well, I don't think X is right [there].*

- give reasons:
  The reason why I … / That's because …
- give examples:
  For example, … / For instance, … / One example of this could be …
- reply to what your partner says in his/her answers.

---

1 🔊 38 **Listen to the two students from Unit 11. Answer the questions.**

1 What are the interlocutor's questions? Write them down.

_____

2 What is the girl's main reason for thinking that young people should have interests outside school?

_____

3 What is the boy's main reason for thinking that young people should have interests outside school?

_____

4 What does the girl think about art lessons in her school?

_____

5 What does the boy think schools should help young people do?

_____

2 **Here are six things that the students say. Write G (girl) or B (boy) in the boxes to show who says them.**

a To my mind ☐	d My own view is that … ☐
b That's because ☐	e Absolutely ☐
c I'm not sure I agree ☐	f I couldn't agree more ☐

3 🔊 38 **Listen again and grade their performance. Circle 1 star for 'could do better', 2 stars for 'good' and 3 stars for 'excellent'.**

	Candidate A (boy)	Candidate B (girl)
Talk relevantly	★ ★★ ★★★	★ ★★ ★★★
Talk for a period of time	★ ★★ ★★★	★ ★★ ★★★
Express their opinions clearly	★ ★★ ★★★	★ ★★ ★★★
Listen to their partner's ideas	★ ★★ ★★★	★ ★★ ★★★

CONSOLIDATION

LISTENING

1 🔊 **39** **Listen to the conversation. Mark and Josie are talking about an urban explorer. Tick the places where he has taken photos.**

a in a train ☐

b in an underground tunnel ☐

c at the top of a bridge ☐

d from a moving car ☐

e in an empty office building ☐

2 🔊 **39** **Listen again. Mark the statements T (true) or F (false).**

1 Josie doesn't know what 'urban exploration' is. ☐

2 The photos in the tunnel were taken in the daytime. ☐

3 The explorer took photos at the top of a railway bridge. ☐

4 Josie thought Mark would be interested in urban exploration. ☐

5 Mark thinks urban exploration would allow him to do different types of photography. ☐

6 The explorer does his exploring on his own. ☐

7 The explorer uses a fictional name on his website. ☐

8 Mark decides he still wants to do urban exploration. ☐

VOCABULARY

3 **Match the sentences.**

1 How often do you see your cousins? ☐

2 So, was the film really exciting? ☐

3 The food was fantastic, wasn't it? ☐

4 How can I help you understand? ☐

5 Hello, can I help you? ☐

6 She's very practical, isn't she? ☐

7 Why shouldn't I swim out there? ☐

8 How come you got wet? ☐

a Yes, it was out of this world.

b Well, give me another example of what you mean.

c Yes, very down to earth.

d Well, there's a dangerous reef just below the surface.

e Oh, only once in a blue moon.

f I got too close to the waterfall.

g Yes. I want to make a complaint.

h Absolutely – it was action-packed.

4 **Circle the correct options.**

1 We've been working all day but we haven't *made / done* much progress.

2 The view from the top of the mountain was *stunning / sentimental*.

3 It was really great news – I was over the *moon / world*.

4 Let's *make / take* advantage of the good weather and go for a walk.

5 Let me *make / give* you some advice.

6 It was really hard to believe – very *far-fetched / down to earth*.

7 Come on, it's easy – it isn't rocket *physics / science*.

8 I need to find a way to *do / make* amends with Charlotte.

GRAMMAR

5 **Rewrite each sentence using the word in brackets. Do not change the word in brackets.**

1 It is possible that they'll come. (MIGHT)

_____

2 He was absent from school. He had a bad cold. (DUE)

_____

3 The earthquake destroyed the house. (BY)

_____

4 I'm 100% sure that he will win. (BOUND)

_____

5 It's not possible that you tried your hardest. (CAN'T)

_____

6 It's probable that there will be bad weather at the weekend. (LIKELY)

_____

7 My grandparents gave me some money. (GIVEN)

_____

8 People think that the president is doing a good job. (THOUGHT)

_____

DIALOGUE

6 Complete the dialogue with the phrases in the list. There are two you won't use.

a shame | the consequences | terrible | don't act
dear | poor | vitally important | pity

DANNY Have you heard they're planning to build a factory near the coast?

FLO No! How ¹_____ ! It'll spoil the coastline completely.

DANNY I know. And I also heard that they're thinking of buying people's houses to make room for it – including my grandmother's house.

FLO ²_____ her!

DANNY So ³_____ are going to be pretty bad I think. If people round here ⁴_____ soon, they'll just go ahead with it. But some people don't seem to care. I tried to talk to some of my friends but they're not interested.

FLO What ⁵_____. I think it's ⁶_____ to do something. Come on, let's sit down and get some ideas together.

DANNY Great. I knew you'd understand, Flo!

READING

7 Read the article and answer the questions.

1 Why did the writer not watch old films in the past?

_____

2 How long has the writer been a fan of sci-fi films?

_____

3 In *Silent Running* there are six domes. What do they contain? _____

4 Who helps Lowell in the domes? _____

5 What order does Lowell decide to disobey?

_____

6 What is the purpose of the fake explosion?

_____

7 How does Lowell try to ensure that the final dome survives? _____

8 Who remains in the last dome?

_____

WRITING

8 Write a paragraph of about 120 words. Write about a sci-fi film you really like or dislike.

Oldie but goldie – *Silent Running*

I don't know about you, but I tend to think that films that are forty or fifty years old aren't going to be all that good – after all, they were mostly made before many of the special effect techniques that we see today were invented. So for a long time, if I saw that a film was made in, say, 1970 or 1980, I'd decide not to watch it. Now, though, I am beginning to realise that I've been making a mistake, because there are some excellent films out there that might not be technically as good as the ones that are released these days, but that have great acting, story-lines and direction. One of these – and here I speak as only a recent convert to sci-fi films – is the 1972 classic *Silent Running*.

It's all set in the future (of course), where all the plants on Earth have become extinct. Some examples of Earth plant life have been put into six huge domes that are like greenhouses, and sent into space, where they are suspended not far from the planet Saturn. The star of the film is Lowell (played by Bruce Dern) who is the botanist in charge of the domes. He's got three people to help him, together with three robots that he nicknames Huey, Dewey and Louie. (As you may recognise, these are named after the three young ducks who are Donald Duck's nephews in cartoon films.)

One day, the people on Earth decide that the domes aren't worth keeping anymore, and Lowell and the others are ordered to destroy them with nuclear bombs. After four of the domes have been blown up, Lowell realises he doesn't want the last two to be destroyed – he decides to disobey the order. He goes to his favourite dome and when the other three men come to blow it up, he kills one of them and traps the other two, but as he does this he hurts his knee very badly.

Then Lowell sets up a fake explosion to make people on Earth think that all the domes have been destroyed. He also gets the robots to do an operation on his knee. After that, he takes the dome on a very dangerous and difficult journey through Saturn's rings. Louie is lost but Lowell and the other two robots get through to the other side. Lowell starts to reprogram the two remaining robots – he teaches them, for example, how to plant trees and how to play card games.

But then a spaceship from Earth arrives to check out what's actually happened. Lowell desperately wants the dome to survive, so he sends it out into space with just Dewey and a watering can on board.

What happens to Lowell? Well, you'll have to watch the film yourself! And it's a great film, so see if you can find it and watch it – I'm sure you won't regret making the effort.

PRONUNCIATION

UNIT 1
Diphthongs: alternative spellings

1   Say the words and write them in the table.

a~~ll~~ow | although | ate | boil | climb | dec<u>i</u>de
enj<u>oy</u> | height | high | hole | how | join
know | loud | noise | shout | straight
tipt<u>oe</u> | wait | weight

/eɪ/ rain	/aɪ/ pie	/əʊ/ coat	/aʊ/ out	/ɔɪ/ boy
			all<u>ow</u>	

2   ◀))03 Listen, check and repeat.

UNIT 2
Phrasal verb stress

1   Tick the sentence in each pair which includes a phrasal verb. Then mark the word you think will be most stressed in each of the underlined phrases for all of the sentences.

0   What are you going to <u>wear to</u> the party?

After PE today we were all <u>worn out</u>! ☑

1   They <u>had to pick a</u> colour for their team. ☐
She <u>picked up</u> French really easily. ☐

2   The cake I made yesterday <u>turned out</u> to be delicious! ☐
Can you <u>turn and</u> face the board, please? ☐

3   I <u>want to hang</u> a picture on that wall. ☐
I always <u>hang out with</u> my friends on Saturdays. ☐

4   Sarah's ill; she's <u>going through</u> a difficult time. ☐
We're <u>going to the</u> city to see a play; would you like to come? ☐

5   I think it's better if we <u>all bring our own</u> food to the party. ☐
Spring <u>brings about</u> many changes in the countryside. ☐

6   I don't know <u>where to put</u> the papers they've left behind. ☐
My neighbours make a lot of noise but I just have to <u>put up with</u> it. ☐

> **Remember:** We stress the particle in a phrasal verb more than the verb because it's very important – it changes the meaning of the verb.

2   ◀))05 Listen, check and repeat.

UNIT 3
Adding emphasis

1   ◀))09 Rewrite the sentences adding so, such, do, does or did. Listen and check your answers.

0   Jack McDonald's a good football player!
Jack McDonald's such a good football player!

1   John gets on well with his parents.
_____

2   We had a fantastic holiday!
_____

3   It may not seem like it, but he likes you.
_____

4   I didn't pass the test – but I studied hard.
_____

5   What a wonderful day – I love it when the sun's shining!
_____

2   Try saying the sentences with and without so, such, do, does and did. What difference do you notice?

3   ◀))09 Listen again and repeat the sentences with so, such, do, does and did.

UNIT 4
Pronouncing words with *gh*

1 **Write the words in the table.**

although | brought | caught | cough | daughter
enough | fight | ghost | height | high | laugh
light | straight | thought | tough | through | weigh

gh silent	*gh* pronounced /f/	*gh* pronounced /g/
although		

2 🔊12 **Listen, check and repeat.**

3 **Match the words in the list that rhyme with words a–l below.**

sport | buy | half | late | off | play | stuff
taught | toast | you | water | white

a	thought	*sport*	g	straight	_____
b	laugh	_____	h	height	_____
c	enough	_____	i	weigh	_____
d	through	_____	j	brought	_____
e	ghost	_____	k	daughter	_____
f	high	_____	l	cough	_____

4 🔊13 **Listen, check and repeat.**

UNIT 5
The schwa sound

1 **Complete the text with the words *to*, *and*, *of*, *for*, *or*, *a* or *an*.**

0 Thank you __*for*__ calling David's telephone service.
1 This is _____ recorded message.
2 There are no operators free to take your call at _____ moment.
3 Press 1 _____ leave a message.
4 Press 2 if you wish to speak to _____ operator.
5 Please don't shout _____ scream at the operators.
6 Now please hang up _____ make yourself a cup _____ tea.

2 🔊16 **Listen, check and repeat.**

3 **Circle the other unstressed words in each sentence which have little meaning and which have the schwa /ə/ sound.**

UNIT 6
Linking words with /dʒ/ and /tʃ/

1 **Complete the sentences with the words in the list. Circle the words linked with the /dʒ/ sound and underline the words linked with a /tʃ/ sound.**

should | can't | could | did | do
don't | just | won't | would

0 There's an extra blanket, (should you) need it.
1 You come from Australia, _____ you?
2 How _____ you learn to paint so well?
3 _____ you like a cup of tea and a biscuit?
4 _____ you know how to do a Sudoku?
5 _____ you move out of the way, please? I can't see the TV.
6 You must be tired after your long walk. _____ you sit down?
7 I haven't told anyone my secret – _____ you.
8 You can swim, _____ you?

2 🔊19 **Listen, check and repeat.**

UNIT 7

Intonation: encouraging someone

1 🔊22 **Listen to the sentences, paying particular attention to the underlined phrases. Does the speaker sound interested (I) or uninterested (U)? Write I or U in the box next to each sentence.**

0   Don't <u>let it get you down</u>. People fail their driving test all the time. | U |

1   Try to <u>look on the bright side</u> – if it's raining we can stay in and watch TV. | |

2   I know <u>you can do it</u>. You just need a few more lessons. | |

3   <u>Don't worry</u> – everything will be fine in the end. | |

4   <u>Cheer up</u>. Things will seem better after a good night's sleep. | |

5   <u>Hang in there</u>. Your exams will be over soon. | |

6   <u>It's not the end of the world</u> – and we've got a day off next week. | |

2 **Repeat the sentences trying to sound interested in all of them.**

UNIT 8

Weak forms with conditionals

1 **Circle the contractions *could've*, *should've* and *would've* where they're pronounced *coulda* /'kʊdə/, *shoulda* /'ʃʊdə/ and *woulda* /'wʊdə/ without the /v/ sound.**

0   I (would've) come if I'd known Kylie was going to be there.

1   You should've seen the waves at the beach yesterday – they were enormous!

2   Sarah could've passed the test but she didn't study for it.

3   Marley would've asked you to help him if he'd known you were free.

4   We didn't know Jack was in hospital – we would've sent a card if we'd known.

5   I should've eaten breakfast – I'm really hungry now!

6   The accident would've been much worse if they'd been driving faster.

7   You could've told me – you knew it was Dad's birthday yesterday!

Remember: You don't have to say the contractions this way – but hearing them will help you understand native speakers better.

2 🔊23 **Listen, check and repeat.**

UNIT 9

Linking: instrusive /w/ and /j/

1 🔊27 **Listen to the sentences and write /w/ or /j/ above the spaces between the underlined words to indicate which intrusive sound you hear.**

                            j
0   My parents tell <u>me off</u> all the time. They're always

        w
    <u>so angry</u> with me!

1   <u>Marie always</u> has a solution <u>to everything</u>.

2   Have <u>you eaten</u> yet? Would you like some <u>tea and</u> biscuits?

3   Do <u>you understand</u> the question? If not, I might <u>be able</u> to help you.

4   I'm <u>so upset</u>! We've lost another match. Why do <u>we always</u> lose?

5   If <u>she ever</u> needs a lift she can come with us. We've got room for <u>two in</u> the back.

6   I don't want to <u>see another</u> film like that. It was <u>too awful</u> for words!

7   <u>I asked</u> Ashley <u>to explain</u> her problem to me.

2 🔊27 **Listen again, check and repeat.**

Remember: You don't have to include the /w/ and /j/ sounds when you speak – but hearing them will help you understand native speakers better.

UNIT 10
Linking: omission of the /h/ sound

1 🔊 30 **Listen to the story and cross out the letter *h* when it's silent.**

Hugo was a hairdresser in a hotel. Harry went to him for a haircut.
Hugo spent an hour cutting Harry's hair. The haircut was horrible and Harry wasn't happy.
He decided to be honest and tell Hugo how he felt.
He didn't want to pay for his haircut.
Hugo was upset because he liked the haircut and he also wanted his money.
In the end, Harry paid him half.

2 🔊 30 **Listen again and check your answers.**

3 **There are two words where the letter *h* is always silent at the beginning. What are they?**

UNIT 11
Stress on modal verbs for speculation

1 🔊 33 **Listen to the pairs of sentences and decide when the speaker thinks it is likely (L) or unlikely (U) that the event will happen or is true. Write 'L' or 'U' in the boxes.**

0 A I just watched a TV show that said aliens <u>might have visited</u> Earth. `U`
   B I just watched a TV show that said aliens <u>might have visited</u> Earth. `L`

1 A I invited Sally and Jack to our party. They said <u>they might come</u>. ☐
   B I invited Sally and Jack to our party. They said <u>they might come</u>. ☐

2 A They say she <u>may win an Oscar</u> for her role in that film. ☐
   B They say she <u>may win an Oscar</u> for her role in that film. ☐

3 A Do you want to try that new restaurant? It <u>could be really good</u>. ☐
   B Do you want to try that new restaurant? It <u>could be really good</u>. ☐

4 A Someone told me that Elvis <u>might still be alive</u>. ☐
   B Someone told me that Elvis <u>might still be alive</u>. ☐

5 A I <u>might become an author</u> when I'm older. ☐
   B I <u>might become an author</u> when I'm older. ☐

2 🔊 33 **Listen again, check and repeat the sentences where the speaker thinks it's likely (L).**

3 🔊 33 **Listen again, check and repeat the sentences where the speaker thinks it's unlikely (U).**

UNIT 12
Linking: intrusive /r/

1 **Read the sentences. Each one contains the intrusive /r/ sound which often links two words that start and end with vowel sounds. Write *r* above the spaces where you think this sound appears. There is one in each sentence.**

                  r

0 Join us on <u>our adventure</u> to faraway places!

1 I don't know why they're angry with us. We didn't do anything wrong!

2 Some animals are finding it harder and harder to live on our planet.

3 From her accent I'd say Julie is French.

4 We're flying into Atlanta airport on our trip to the USA.

5 It's another awful day – I wish it wasn't raining again!

6 I'd like to go to Australia and America when I'm older.

7 Hannah always leaves her homework until the last minute.

2 🔊 37 **Listen, check and repeat.**

> **Remember:** You don't have to include the /r/ sounds when you speak – but hearing it will help you understand native speakers better.

GRAMMAR REFERENCE

UNIT 1

Verb patterns: *to* + infinitive or gerund

1   When a verb is followed by another verb, the second verb is either in the gerund form (*-ing*) or it is an infinitive with *to*.

2   These verbs are followed by a gerund: *imagine, feel like, suggest, practise, miss, can't stand, enjoy, detest,* and *don't mind*.

   *I **enjoy cooking** but I **can't stand washing** the dishes.*

3   These verbs are followed by an infinitive with *to*: *decide, refuse, hope, promise, ask, expect, afford, offer* and *choose*.

   *I can't **afford to buy** a new smart phone.*

4   These verbs can be followed by either form with no difference in meaning: *begin, start, continue*.

   *We **started walking** / **to walk** towards the town.*
   *It **continued raining** / **to rain** until late afternoon.*

Verbs + gerund and *to* + infinitive with different meanings

The verbs *remember, try, stop, regret, forget* can be followed by either form (gerund or infinitive) but with a difference in meaning. The difference relates to time: which action came first (1) and which came second (2). In general, verb + gerund looks back, and verb + infinitive looks forward.

Remember

*I **remember going** there last year. (I went last year (1) and some time later, I remembered (2))*
*I **remembered to go** to the supermarket. (First I remembered (1) and then I went (2))*

Forget

*I'll never **forget meeting** you. (First I met you (1) and now I won't forget (2))*
*Don't **forget to meet** me at the cinema. (First don't forget (1) and then meet me at the cinema (2))*

Stop

*We **stopped eating** and left the café. (First we ate (1) and then we stopped (2))*
*We **stopped to eat** our sandwiches. (First we stopped (1) and then we ate (2))*

Try

*I **tried taking** the medicine but I still felt ill. (I felt ill. I took the medicine. After the medicine, I didn't feel better.)*
*I **tried to take** the medicine but I couldn't swallow it. (= I wanted to take the medicine, but I was unsuccessful.)*

Regret

*I really **regret telling** him what happened. (First I told him what happened (1) I am sorry that I told him (2))*
*I **regret to tell** you that you failed the exam. (You failed (1) and I'm sorry to have to tell you this (2))*

UNIT 2

Relative clauses (review)

1   A defining relative clause identifies the thing, person, place or possession that we are talking about. We do not use a comma in these clauses.

   *The woman **who** gives the lectures is very intelligent. (= There is only one woman who gives the lectures.)*
   *The city **where** I grew up is a great place. (= I am talking about the only city where I grew up.)*

2   A non-defining relative clause gives additional information about the thing, person, place or possession we are talking about. This information is between commas.

   *The woman, **who** gives the lectures, is very intelligent. (= I am talking about an intelligent woman and adding the non-essential information that she gives lectures.)*
   *The city, **where** I grew up, is a great place. (= I am talking about a city that's a great place, and adding that it is where I grew up.)*

which to refer to a whole clause

When we want to refer back to a clause or an idea, we use the relative pronoun *which* (not ~~that~~ or ~~what~~)

*He had to go out and find a job, **which** wasn't easy.*
*This phone is very good, **which** is why it's so popular.*

Omitting relative pronouns and reduced relative clauses

1   When the relative pronouns *that / which / who* are the object of the following clause, they can be omitted. They can't be omitted when they are the subject of the following clause.

   *He's the man (**that**) I told you about.*
   *He's the boy **who** sold me this watch.*

2 When the relative pronoun is followed by the verb *be*, we can leave out both the relative pronoun and the verb *be*. This is called a 'reduced relative clause'.

*Their house, (**which was**) built only last year, was completely destroyed by the tornado.*
*The people (**who are**) running the company are not doing their job properly.*

UNIT 3
Quantifiers

1 Quantifiers are words that we use to say how many or how much of a noun. Frequent quantifiers are:

none, hardly any, a few / a little, (not) many / much, some, several, most, a lot / lots, loads, all

2 The quantifiers *a few / (not) many / several* are only used with countable nouns. The quantifiers *a little / (not) much* are only used with uncountable nouns.

*I've been to **a few / many / several** rock **concerts**.*
*They took **a little food** on the trip.*
*They didn't take **much food** on the trip.*

3 Some quantifiers always need the word *of* before the noun or pronoun they refer to:

***None of** the books were cheap.*
***A lot of** people think that way.*

4 All the quantifiers need the word *of* when they are followed by a pronoun:

*Hardly any films are made here, and **hardly any of them** are good.*
*There is some food in the fridge, but **some of it** is quite old.*

5 The word *none (of)* is grammatically singular but many people use a plural verb after it.

*I've got lots of friends, but **none of** them **are** musicians.*

so and such (review)

1 We use the words *so* and *such* to emphasise what we are saying:

*This food is **so** delicious!   She's **such** a good writer.*

2 We use *so* + adjective. We use *such* (+ adjective) + noun (or pronoun).

*The weather's **so** good.   It's **such** a wonderful day.*

3 We can follow these phrases with a *that* clause, to show consequences.

*The weather was so good **that** we went for a walk.*
*It was such good weather **that** we went for a walk.*

do and did for emphasis

We can use the auxiliary verb *do / does* (or *did* in the past) to emphasise the verb.

*I **did like** the food! I just wasn't very hungry.*
*We didn't have time to go to the museum, but we **did go** to the park.*

UNIT 4
be / get used to (doing) vs. used to (do)

1 When we want to talk about something being normal or familiar, we can use the expression *be used to*.

*It's cold where I live, so I**'m used to wearing** a lot of warm clothes.*

2 We use *get used to* to refer to the process of something becoming normal or familiar.

*It took him a while to **get used to eating** dinner early.*

3 These expressions are followed by a noun or the gerund (*-ing*) form of a verb.

*I'm not really **used to** spicy **food**.*
*They've **got used to living** in a small apartment.*

4 These expressions are not the same as *used to*, which refers to past habits or states which are no longer true and is followed by an infinitive without *to*.

*I **used to love** their music, but now I never listen to it.*

Adverbs and adverbial phrases

Adverbs qualify verbs. They can qualify verbs in different ways, for example:

Adverbs of manner (*how*)	He walked **quickly**.
Adverbs of time (*when*)	We got there **late**.
Adverbs of place (*where*)	Sign **here**, please.
Adverbs of probability	You **probably** think I'm crazy!
Adverbs of opinion	It's **surprisingly** quiet in here.

We can also use adverbial phrases to describe a verb and to say how an action is/was performed.

One structure for adverbial phrases is with + noun.

*When I told her, she reacted **with surprise**.*

Another structure for adverbial phrases is in a(n) + adjective + way.

*Our teacher explains things **in a fun way**.*

Adverbial phrases are often used when an adjective (e.g. *friendly, difficult, interesting, fun*) has no adverb form.

UNIT 5

Obligation, permission and prohibition (review)

1 We can talk about obligation and necessity by using *must, have to* and *(be) supposed to.*

   *You **must** get there before eight o'clock.* (= This is an obligation imposed by the speaker.)
   *We **have to** finish our projects by Friday.* (= This is an obligation imposed by someone else.)
   *We're **supposed to** switch off our phones in lessons.* (= This is the rule, but we don't always follow it.)

2 We can talk about no obligation or no necessity by using *don't have to* and *don't need to.*

   *You **don't have to** eat this if you don't want to.*
   *We **didn't need to** buy tickets – my dad gave us some.*

3 We can say something is (or isn't) a good idea by using *should(n't).*

   *You **should** leave now if you don't want to miss your bus.*
   *I **shouldn't** eat any more or I'll feel sick.*

4 We can talk about permission using *let* or *be allowed to. Let* is active voice, while *be allowed to* is passive voice.

   *The school **lets** us use the tennis courts at the weekend.*
   *We're **allowed to** use the tennis courts at the weekend.*

5 We can talk about prohibition using *(not) be allowed to* or *don't/doesn't let.* When we don't know, or don't want to say who it is that prohibits something, we use 'they'.

   *Cyclists **are not allowed to** leave their bikes here.*
   *They **don't let** cyclists leave their bikes here.*

Necessity: *(didn't) need to / needn't have*

We use *didn't need to* and *needn't have* to talk about the past necessity of actions. There is a small but important difference between the structures.

1 *didn't need to* usually suggests that we didn't do something because it wasn't necessary.

   *I **didn't need to** go to the doctor.* (I didn't go.)

2 *needn't have* means that we did something but actually it wasn't necessary.

   *We **needn't have** cooked all this food – only four people turned up at the party.* (We cooked a lot of food but it wasn't necessary.)

Ability in the past: *could, was/were able to, managed to, succeeded in doing*

1 When we talk about ability in the past, we can use *could/couldn't, managed to, was/were able to* or *succeeded (in doing).* However, there are differences between them.

2 We use *could / couldn't* to talk about general ability in the past.

   *My brother **couldn't ride** a bike until he was twelve.*
   *I **could do** maths in my head when I was a kid.*

3 When we want to talk about no ability on a specific occasion in the past, we have three possibilities:

   *I listened, but I **couldn't hear** anything.*
   *I worked hard, but I **didn't manage to finish** everything.*
   *I hurt my leg and I **wasn't able to walk** for two weeks.*

4 But, when we want to talk about ability on a specific occasion in the past, we don't use *could*:

   *The wall was very high but we **managed to climb** over it.* (NOT: *we could climb over it.*)
   *Because we bought our tickets a long time in advance, we **were able to get** them quite cheaply.* (NOT: *we could get them …*)

5 We use *succeeded (in doing)* to emphasise that something was difficult in the past but we were able to do it.

   *I had to wait for hours, but I **succeeded in getting** tickets.*

UNIT 6

Comparatives

1 We can intensify a comparison (make it stronger) using *a lot / far / much* + comparative adjective.

   *Use a calculator – it's **far easier** that way.*
   *Let's take a taxi, it's **much quicker.***
   *It's **a lot more difficult** than I thought.*

2 Comparisons with *as … as* can be made stronger with *not nearly* or *nowhere near.*

   *He's **not nearly as clever as** his sister.* (His sister is much cleverer than him.)
   *The film is **nowhere near as good as** the book.* (The book is far better than the film.)

3 We can use *just* with *as … as* to emphasise how similar two things are.

   *Our team is **just as good as** yours.* (The two teams are really equally good.)

4 We can use comparative *and* comparative with short adjectives or *more and more* + adjective with longer adjectives to show how comparisons become stronger over time.

*My little sister's getting **bigger and bigger** every day.*
*Train tickets are getting **more and more expensive**.*

5 We can use *the* + comparative (+ clause), *the* + comparative (+ clause) with short adjectives, or *the more* … adjective (+ clause), *the more* … adjective (+ clause) with longer adjectives, to show how two events affect each other.

***The longer** I sat there, **the more uncomfortable** I became.*
***The older** people are, **the more interesting** they are.*

Linkers of contrast

1 The linkers *although* and *even though* are followed by a clause. They can be used at the beginning of a sentence, or before the second clause.

*I passed my driving test, **although / even though** I made some mistakes.*
***Although / Even though** I made some mistakes in my driving test, I passed.*

2 The linkers *despite* and *in spite of* are followed by a noun phrase or a gerund. They can be used at the beginning of a sentence, or before the second clause.

*I passed my driving test, **despite / in spite of** (making) some mistakes.*
***Despite** (making) some mistakes in my driving test, I passed.*

3 The linkers *however* and *nevertheless* come at the beginning of a sentence and introduce a contrast with what was said in the previous sentence.

*I made some mistakes in my driving test. **However** / **Nevertheless**, I passed.*

UNIT 7
Ways of referring to the future (review)

Some common ways to refer to the future include:

1 *be going to* for plans, intentions and evidence-based predictions

*I**'m going to visit** my grandparents tomorrow.*

2 *will* for future facts, spontaneous decisions and offers, and feeling-based predictions

*Technology **will develop** a lot in the next twenty years.*

3 the present continuous for arrangements

*We**'re taking** our cat to the vet this afternoon.*

4 the present simple for events that are part of a timetable, and after time expressions like *when, before, after, until*, and *as soon as*

*I'll meet you when you **arrive** tomorrow.*

Future continuous and future perfect

1 The future continuous is formed by *will* + *be* + *-ing* form of the verb.

2 We use the future continuous tense to talk about an action that will be in progress at a specified future time.

*When I'm 25, I**'ll be living** in another country.*

3 The future perfect tense is formed by *will* + *have* + the past participle of the verb.

4 We use the future perfect tense to talk about an action that we think will be completed by a specified future time.

*By 2025, the population **will have grown** enormously.*

UNIT 8
Conditionals (review)

1 We use the zero conditional to talk about a condition and its consequence that are always true.

*If I **go** running, I always **feel** better.*

2 We use the first conditional to talk about a condition and its possible future consequence.

*If you **make** a list, you**'ll remember** what you need.*

3 We use the second conditional to talk about a hypothetical situation in the present.

*If I **had** more time, I**'d take up** the guitar.*

4 We use the third conditional to talk about an imaginary situation in the past and its consequence in the past which is impossible to change.

*If we **had left** earlier, we **wouldn't have been** late.*

Mixed conditionals

Conditional sentences don't always follow the four patterns described above. It's possible to mix second and third conditionals.

1 If we want to talk about an imaginary / unreal past action and its present consequence, then the *if* clause follows the pattern of a third conditional and the consequence clause follows the pattern of a second conditional.

*If I**'d paid** more attention in class, I**'d know** how to do this exercise. (I didn't pay attention. I don't know how to do this exercise.)*

2 If we want to talk about how a hypothetical or imaginary present could or would change the past, then the *if* clause follows the pattern of a second conditional and the consequence clause follows the pattern of a third conditional.

*If I **had** more self-confidence, I **would have gone** and talked to him. (I didn't go and talk to him, because I don't have much self-confidence.)*

UNIT 9
I wish and if only

1 We can use *I wish* or *if only* to talk about how we would like things to be different now or in the future. The verb that follows *I wish / if only* is in the past simple tense.

*I wish I **knew** her name. (I don't know her name and I'm sorry about that.)*
*If only I **could** stay in bed a bit longer. (I can't stay in bed longer, but I want to!)*

2 We can also use *I wish* or *if only* to talk about regrets we have about the past. In this case, the verb that follows *I wish / if only* is in the past perfect tense.

*I wish you**'d told** me about it before.*
*If only I **hadn't missed** that penalty.*

I would prefer to / it if; It's time; I'd rather / sooner

1 To talk about our own preferences, we can use *I'd prefer + to* infinitive, or we can use *I'd rather / I'd sooner* + base form. *I'd rather* is far more common than *I'd sooner*.

*I'd **prefer to stay** home tonight.*
*I'd **rather / I'd sooner have** fish than chicken for dinner.*

2 To say what we would like another person to do, we can use *I'd rather / I'd sooner* + subject + past simple tense, or we can use *I'd prefer it if* + subject + past simple tense.

*I'd rather **you phoned** me tomorrow, if that's OK.*
*I'd prefer it if **my friends didn't make** fun of me.*

3 We can use *It's time* + subject + past simple to say that we think someone should do something (and to suggest that it should be done immediately).

*It's time **we left**. (We should leave now.)*

UNIT 10
Reported speech (review)

1 When we report what someone said, there is often a change in verb tense between the direct speech (what the person actually said) and the indirect (reported) speech.

*'Someone**'s eaten** all the food!' he said.*	→	*He said someone **had eaten** all the food.*
*'I **can't** do this,' he said.*	→	*He said he **couldn't** do it.*

2 If the information in the direct speech is still true, we don't necessarily need to change the verb tense.

*'He**'s** hopeless,' she told me.*	→	*She told me he**'s** hopeless.*

Reported questions and requests

1 When we report a *yes/no* question, we use *if* or *whether* and normal word order (subject + verb).

'Do you know this song?' → *She asked me **if I knew** the song. (NOT: She asked me did I know …)*

2 When we report *wh-* questions, we use the same question word and normal word order (subject + verb).

'Where did they go?' → *He asked me **where they'd gone**. (NOT: He asked me where did they go)*

3 When we report a request or order, we use *asked* + person + *to* + infinitive

'Please help me.' → *He **asked me to help** him.*

Verb patterns

There are many verbs that we can use to report what people said. Each one tells us what kind of thing was said (e.g. a demand, a threat, a warning, an apology, etc.). There are different patterns that follow the verbs.

The most frequent patterns are:

1 + [person] + infinitive, e.g. *tell / ask / warn / order / advise / persuade*
*They asked **us to leave**.*

2 + *to* + infinitive OR + *that* clause, e.g. *agree*
*He agreed **to go**.*
*He agreed **that** it was a bad idea.*

3 + gerund OR + that clause, e.g. *admit / regret / deny / suggest*
*They suggested **walking**.*
*They admitted **that** it was a good thing to do.*

4 + person + *of* + gerund, e.g. *accuse*
*He accused **me of taking** his things without asking.*

UNIT 11
Speculating (past, present and future)

We often use the modal verbs *might / may / could / must / can't* to speculate about the present, the past or the future.

1 We use *might / may / could* to talk about a possibility.

   She *might / may / could* be Mexican.

2 We use *must* when we want to say that we are certain, based on evidence.

   You're going swimming in the sea in winter? You *must be crazy!*

3 We use *can't* when we believe something is impossible, based on evidence.

   There's no one in that restaurant – it *can't* be very good.

4 When we speculate about the past, we use the modal verb + *have* + past participle.

   Everyone is talking about the film last night – it *must have been* very good.
   I'm surprised John wasn't at the party – he was really looking forward to it. He *must have been* sick.

5 We can also use *be + bound to / certain to / likely to* to speculate about present and future events. The expression *be likely to* is not as sure as *be bound to / be certain to.*

   Ask Jo, she's really smart, so she's *bound to* know.
   The weather forecast says it*'s likely to* rain later today.

Cause and effect linkers

We use the linkers *due to / as a result of / because of / consequently* to link actions and their consequences.

1 We use *because of / due to / as a result of* before the reason for an action or event. These phrases can come at the beginning of a sentence, or in the middle. They are usually followed by a noun or noun phrase.

   The government changed its mind *because of / due to / as a result of* pressure from the population.
   Because of / Due to / As a result of pressure from the population, the government changed its mind.

2 The word *consequently* introduces the result of a previous idea. It is usually used at the beginning of a new sentence.

   Sales of the new car were very low. *Consequently*, the company lowered the price for a few weeks.

UNIT 12
Passive report structures

1 We use passive report structures when we want to report information and the agent is not important.

   The Amazon rainforest *is known to be* the largest forest in the world. (It is not important to say who thinks this.)

2 We mostly use passive report structures with verbs like *say, think, believe, know* and *consider.*

3 If we use a passive report structure to talk about beliefs or knowledge in the present we use *be +* past participle of the reporting verb + infinitive.

   Really strange creatures *are thought to exist* in the deep oceans.
   She *is considered to be* a real expert on wildlife.

4 If we use a passive report structure to talk about beliefs or knowledge in the past, we use *be +* past participle of the reporting verb + *to* + present perfect infinitive.

   Dinosaurs *are thought to have disappeared* because of a major disaster on Earth. (They no longer exist.)
   They *are known to have had* very small brains.

5 Passive report structures are quite formal and are commonly used in news reports.

The passive: verbs with two objects

1 Some verbs (like *give, offer, ask, promise, read, show, write*, etc.) have two possible passive forms. This is because these verbs can be followed by two objects – a person and a thing.

2 The two possible active forms are:

   a) verb + indirect object + direct object: *Someone gave me a present.*
   b) verb + direct object + indirect object: *Someone gave a present to me.*

3 The two possible passive constructions are:

   a) *I was given a present.* (The person is the subject of the sentence.)
   b) *A present was given to me.* (The thing is the subject of the sentence.)

4 It is more usual to have the person as the subject of the passive construction (as in 3a) not the thing (as in 3b).

   The kids were shown a film is more likely than *A film was shown to the kids.*

IRREGULAR VERBS

Base form	Past simple	Past participle
be	was / were	been
bear	bore	borne
beat	beat	beaten
become	became	become
begin	began	begun
bend	bent	bent
bet	bet	bet
bite	bit	bit
blow	blew	blown
break	broke	broken
breed	bred	bred
bring	brought	brought
broadcast	broadcast	broadcast
build	built	built
burn	burned / burnt	burned / burnt
buy	bought	bought
can	could	–
catch	caught	caught
choose	chose	chosen
come	came	come
cost	cost	cost
cut	cut	cut
deal	dealt	dealt
dive	dived / dove	dived
do	did	done
draw	drew	drawn
dream	dreamed / dreamt	dreamed / dreamt
drink	drank	drunk
drive	drove	driven
eat	ate	eaten
fall	fell	fallen
feed	fed	fed
feel	felt	felt
fight	fought	fought
find	found	found
flee	fled	fled
fly	flew	flown
forbid	forbade	forbidden
forget	forgot	forgotten
forgive	forgave	forgiven
freeze	froze	frozen
get	got	got
give	gave	given
go	went	gone
grow	grew	grown
hang	hung	hung
have	had	had
hear	heard	heard
hide	hid	hid
hit	hit	hit
hold	held	held
hurt	hurt	hurt
keep	kept	kept
know	knew	known
lay	laid	laid
lead	led	led
learn	learned / learnt	learned / learnt
leave	left	left

Base form	Past simple	Past participle
lend	lent	lent
let	let	let
lie	lay / laid	laid
light	lit	lit
lose	lost	lost
make	made	made
mean	meant	meant
meet	met	met
misunderstand	misunderstood	misunderstood
overcome	overcame	overcome
pay	paid	paid
put	put	put
quit	quit	quit
read /riːd/	read /red/	read /red/
ride	rode	ridden
ring	rang	rung
rise	rose	risen
run	ran	run
say	said	said
see	saw	seen
seek	sought	sought
sell	sold	sold
send	sent	sent
set	set	set
shake	shook	shaken
shine	shone	shone
shoot	shot	shot
show	showed	shown
shut	shut	shut
sing	sang	sung
sink	sank	sunk
sit	sat	sat
sleep	slept	slept
speak	spoke	spoken
speed	sped	sped
spend	spent	spent
spill	spilled / spilt	spilled / spilt
split	split	split
spread	spread	spread
stand	stood	stood
steal	stole	stolen
stick	stuck	stuck
strike	struck	struck
swear	swore	sworn
sweep	swept	swept
swim	swam	swum
swing	swung	swung
take	took	taken
teach	taught	taught
tear	tore	torn
tell	told	told
think	thought	thought
throw	threw	thrown
understand	understood	understood
wake	woke	woken
wear	wore	worn
win	won	won
write	wrote	written